Little Women

A Play

Peter Clapham

Adapted from the novel by
Louisa M. Alcott

Samuel French – London
New York – Sydney – Toronto – Hollywood

CHARACTERS

Amy March
Beth March
Jo March
Meg March
Hannah
Mrs March (Marmee)
Aunt March
Laurie
John Brooke
Mr Laurence
Mr March

The action of the play passes in the parlour of the home of the March family on the outskirts of Concord, a small town in Massachusetts, New England, in the 1860s, during the American Civil War.

ACT I   Scene 1   A few days before Christmas—late afternoon

            Scene 2   New Year's Eve—early evening

            Scene 3   The following afternoon

ACT II   Scene 1   The following summer—later afternoon

            Scene 2   The following day—about the same time

ACT III Scene 1   November of the same year—a Sunday morning

            Scene 2   Ten days later—late evening

            Scene 3   Christmas morning—about noon

LITTLE WOMEN

First presented at the Palace Avenue Theatre, Paignton, on the 26th January 1960, with the following cast:

Amy March	Anne Bushell
Jo March	Brenda Simpson
Meg March	Pauline Bellamy
Beth March	Sadie Bonstow
Hannah	Peggy Risely
Mrs March (Marmee)	Audrey Miller
Aunt March	Elizabeth Heslop
Laurie	Michael Tearle
John Brooke	Bruce Kent
Mr Laurence	Howard Baker
Dr Bangs	Peter Pitman
Mr March	Clive Baily

Directed by Peter Clapham

INTRODUCTION

Louisa May Alcott published her first book, a volume of short stories, in 1854 at the age of twenty-two, but it was not until fourteen years later that the March family made their début in her most successful novel, *Little Women*. Written during the summer of 1868 at Orchard House, the Alcott home in Concord, Massachusetts, it chronicled to a large degree actual events that had happened to her and her family in their youth.

Her own life was not an easy one, and, for much of the time, she was the main support of her family, but throughout difficult days and happier times one of her greatest pleasures was always the theatre. She delighted in the performances of all the famous actors and actresses of her day—Laura Keene, John Gilbert, Clara Morris, the Booths and Fanny Kemble—whom she always went to see whenever they visited nearby Boston, or when she herself was in New York.

Later, when the success of *Little Women* had brought her fame, fortune and international prestige, she was fêted in fashionable drawing-rooms everywhere. In these surroundings she was able to meet, at first hand and on an equal footing, some of the theatrical personalities she had before been able to admire only from afar. In 1883 she joined the literary great of the time to meet Ellen Terry on a visit to Boston, and the year before had been guest of honour at a reception in New York to welcome the young Oscar Wilde. They must have made an oddly contrasted pair—the unsophisticated spinster from New England, discreetly dressed in black, and the exuberant exhibitionist from the Old Country, also in black, but sporting knee-breeches, sparkling buckles, diamond studs and luxuriant curls falling to his shoulders.

From childhood an enthusiastic amateur actress and stage director, she had also written numerous pieces for both family plays and the various amateur dramatic societies with whom she worked. This area of her early life she included with loving detail in her story of the Marches. These plays were full-length with, in the fashion of the times, title, sub-title and fourteen scenes. Their themes seem to have been largely melodramatic if we are to judge by titles such as *Norna; or the Witch's Curse* (a sub-title which she later used for one of Jo's plays in *Little Women*), or *The Captive of Castile*; but she had also a great affection for the novels of Charles Dickens from whose work she dramatised selections which she called *Scenes from Dickens*.

As an actress her forte seems, rather surprisingly, to have been broad comedy roles such as Widow Pottle, in Planché's *The Jacobite*, and Mrs O'Scuttle in *Poor Pillicoddy*, though, on one occasion, she did rise to the dizzy heights of Mrs Malaprop in *The Rivals*. She was particularly taken by Mrs Jarley in *The Old Curiosity Shop*, and dramatised the episode of the waxworks to make a monologue for herself to which she returned repeatedly when asked to do charity performances.

With such an active and varied interest in the theatre, it seems more than likely that Louisa Alcott would rejoice in a stage version of her most famous book. Certainly, audiences everywhere have rejoiced across the years. There has been more than one adaptation for the theatre, as well as film versions and television series.

This adaptation has been presented regularly all over the United Kingdom, and elsewhere in the English-speaking world, since it was first produced in 1960. In this country it has been given national tours with star-names, numerous repertory productions and many more amateur productions. Like the original novel, its appeal seems as fresh as ever, and, whether it has been a polished, professional version in a large theatre or a much simpler production in a village hall, audiences have received it with warmth and enthusiasm.

Ivan Butler has paid it the compliment of including it in his book, *The Hundred Best Full-Length Plays for Amateurs*, and in 1972 it was accorded the greatest compliment of all when this version was chosen to be presented in Concord to celebrate the one hundred and fortieth anniversary of Louisa Alcott's birth.

New editions of the novel appear each year, and its enduring charm seems to capture the imagination of modern readers as firmly as those who took the March family to their hearts when they made their first appearance in 1868. Intended originally as a book for younger readers, with whom it was an instant and lasting success, it was also acclaimed by all ages of general reader. Copies sold by the tens of thousands, and in the following year it made its first appearance in England—again with immediate success.

Into this tale of a year in the life of a New England family Louisa Alcott had woven so much of her own earlier life and that of her family—everyone with the exception of Aunt March had a prototype—that fact and fiction grew firmly together to create a domestic novel which went far beyond its setting. Despite the fact that one critic deplored the lack of Christian religion in it, and declared it to be 'no good book for the Sunday-school library', contemporary comment in general acclaimed it as a truthful picture of American home-life. However, a wider appeal soon made itself felt, the secret of which lies, perhaps, in the fact that it is something more than just an American story; it has a universal quality drawing readers and audiences alike, irrespective of time and place, to identify with both the characters and the situations.

A family story is a classic format which rarely fails with audiences as countless plays, films and television serials using this theme continue to prove. Furthermore, in this instance, what was once a contemporary novel has, with the passage of time, now acquired the golden glow of a period piece—evoking a nostalgia for the charm of yesteryear and those salad days when everything seemed simpler, kinder and more clearly defined.

There are those who will always find it too sentimental for their taste, but the fact remains that it continues to enchant successive generations of new devotees.

In the United States *Little Women* appears as a two-volume novel; in the United Kingdom it is published as two books—*Little Women* and *Good Wives*. This adaptation covers only *Little Women* as it is known in this country; there seemed more than enough material and incident to form the basis of a play, and I subsequently adapted *Good Wives* into a sequel. Occasionally, someone, confusing the two books, will query why Beth still survives at the end of the play; her sad demise takes place, of course, in *Good Wives*. This third edition has been extensively revised and, in some places, re-written to make a tighter script with a reduced running time. One character from the earlier editions has been removed—that of the doctor whose appearance was not essential to the plot. Otherwise, my endeavour has remained the same—quite simply, to be true to Louisa Alcott's original novel; many well-remembered incidents have had to be left out, but the continuing popularity of the play encourages the conclusion that the essential charm of the story and its characters have moved successfully from page to stage.

Peter Clapham
February 1986

ACT I*

SCENE 1

The parlour of the March family. Late afternoon

The parlour is a large, comfortable room. There is a fireplace DR *and a large bay-window* UL *which overlooks a pleasant, informal garden and the path to the front door. A draped archway at the back leads to a hallway in which can be seen the foot of a staircase leading to the upper floor. Off* L *in the hallway, but out of sight, is the front door and a door to the dining-room on the other side of the house; off* R *leads to the kitchen and the back of the house. The furnishings are good and include several graceful pieces, but the drapes and carpets are all a little worn and faded for the family have known both better times and financial hardship. However the room is well-cared for and looks warmly inviting with its books, pictures, ornaments and potted plants. The original novel describes it as being pervaded by "a pleasant atmosphere of home peace"*

The play opens a few days before Christmas and the room has been decorated with holly and evergreens. In the bay-window stands a Christmas tree bright with ribbons, tinsel and little silver ornaments

The CURTAIN *rises in darkness and the Lights come up gently on the four March sisters*

Meg, the eldest, a pretty, good-natured girl who, feeling she is a much more mature young lady than her sisters, expresses it in a growing awareness of her clothes and appearance, is seated by the fire industriously knitting a man's dark-blue sock

Jo, the tomboy of the family, only a year younger, "rapidly shooting up into a woman" and not liking it, is stretched out moodily on the hearth-rug turning the pages of a book. She is not the beauty of the family, and her coltish manner and movements do little to add to her femininity. Her best feature is her long, thick hair which, at the moment, she has bundled up into a net at the nape of her neck to be out of her way

Beth, the gentlest and shyest of the four, stands, bright-eyed and patient, holding a box of decorations from which Amy, the youngest, the prettiest

---

*N.B. Paragraph 3 on page ii of this Acting Edition regarding photocopying and video-recording should be carefully read.

and—in her opinion at least—the most important, is putting the finishing touches to the Christmas tree

Amy puts the last silver star in place and regards her handiwork with great satisfaction

Amy There, that's done!

Beth It looks lovely, Amy. Now we're all ready for Christmas!

Jo (*moodily*) Christmas won't be Christmas without any presents. And, even worse, Father's away at the war and won't be able to get home.

Meg (*gently*) We don't really have the money to spend on presents this year, Jo, but we do have each other and Mother to look after us.

Beth And dear old Hannah.

Meg Yes, we've lots to be thankful for.

Jo (*turning a page, unconvinced*) Humph!

Amy puts the Christmas decoration box away

Amy (*a little self-righteously*) Marmee says it's going to be a hard winter for everyone, and she thinks that we ought not to spend money for pleasure when our men in the army are suffering so. She says it's our way of making some sort of sacrifice, and we ought to do it gladly . . . (*pausing briefly as she faces reality*) but I'm afraid I don't.

Jo I can't see that the little we should spend would do any good. (*Sitting up*) Look, we've each got a dollar, and the army wouldn't be helped by our giving that. I agree not to expect anything from Marmee or you, but there is a book I've wanted to buy for ages.

Amy Oh, you and your old books! You never think of anything else! I was going to get some drawing pencils with my dollar; I really need them.

Beth (*rather ashamed of admitting it*) And I'd planned to spend mine on some new piano music.

Pause. Four consciences take a step backward

Meg (*a little uncertainly*) Well, I don't suppose Mother would want us to give up everything . . .

Jo (*decisively*) Let's each buy what we want and have a little fun. I'm sure we work hard enough to earn it.

Meg I know *I* do—teaching those tiresome children of Mrs King's all day!

Jo Being a governess isn't half as bad as being shut up for hours on end as a companion to Aunt March! There never was such a tiresome old fuss-pot!

Beth I don't know how you cope with her, Jo. She just frightens me to death. I'm glad I have only to stay at home and help.

Jo Oh, she keeps me on the trot, I can tell you, and she's never satisfied. Then, every day I have to read to her—and what do I have to read? It's always the same—those odious essays of Mr Belsham. When I think of all the wonderful books Aunt March could buy with all the money she has. But, no! We just read, read and re-read Mr Belsham's boring old book!

Beth It's wrong to grumble, I know, but I do think washing dishes and keeping things clean and tidy home here is just the worst work in the world. My hands get so stiff that I can't practise well at the piano at all.

Amy I don't believe any of you suffer as I do for you don't have to go to school. It's such a *deggerregration* to have to mix with impertinent girls who laugh at your dresses because they're not new, and insult you when your nose isn't nice, and *label* your father because he isn't rich.

Jo If you mean *libel*, I'd say so, and not talk about *labels* as if Father was a jar of pickles.

Amy I know what I mean, and you needn't be *statirical* about it. It's proper to use words, and improve your *vocabulary*. Anyway I don't use slang words like you.

Jo starts to whistle

And I don't whistle either. It's so boyish.

Jo That's why I do it.

Amy I detest rude, unladylike girls!

Jo And I hate affected, niminy-piminy chits!

Meg Jo! Amy! Don't peck at one another! Josephine, you are old enough to leave off boyish tricks and behave better. It didn't matter so much when you were a little girl, but now you are older and turn up your hair you should remember that you are a young lady.

Jo I'm not! And if turning up my hair makes me one then I'll wear it in two tails till I'm thirty! (*She pulls off her hair net and shakes her hair out*) I hate to think I've got to grow up and be "Miss March". It's bad enough to be a girl anyway. (*She collects her knitting from a workbasket on the table*) I can't get over my disappointment in not being a boy; and it's worse than ever now. I'm dying to go and fight with Father, but I can only stay at home and knit like a poky old woman! (*She flops into a chair and starts to knit*)

Beth (*going to Jo*) Poor Jo! It's too bad, but it can't be helped, so you must try to be content with making your name boyish, and playing brother to us girls.

Meg As for you, Amy, you are altogether too particular and prim. Your airs are funny now; but you'll grow up an affected goose if you don't take care. It is good to cultivate nice manners and a refined way of speaking, but your absurd words are quite as bad as Jo's slang.

Beth (*trying to brighten the situation*) If Jo is a tomboy and Amy a goose, what am I?

Meg You're a dear and nothing else.

The clock on the mantelpiece begins to strike six

Six o'clock! Mother will be here at any minute and nothing ready for her—oh, dear, what a self-pitying, bickery lot we are! Come along, let's put things to rights and have everything ready for her when she comes in.

There is a good-natured bustle as the girls tidy the room for their mother's return. Jo adjusts the chair in which Meg has been sitting. Meg packs up the knitting. Beth fetches an extra cushion

Amy fetches her mother's slippers to warm them by the fire

Amy These slippers of Marmee's are quite worn out. She needs a new pair badly.

Pause. Four consciences are pricked

Beth I think I'll get her some for Christmas with my dollar.
Amy No, I will!
Meg I'm the eldest, so I think that ...
Jo (*cutting in*) I am the man of the family now Father is away, and I shall provide the slippers, for he told me to take special care of Mother while he was gone.
Beth I'll tell you what we'll do! Let's each get her something for Christmas and not get anything for ourselves. We don't deserve anything sitting around at home grumbling when Marmee has been down at the Soldiers Aid Society working hard all day.
Meg Beth is quite right—we ought to be ashamed of ourselves. I think I shall give Mother some gloves; she has only two pairs and they are both very darned.

Their voices rise to a loud babble as they all talk at once

Amy I shall give her a nice bottle of cologne.
Beth I did see some pretty handkerchiefs in town which would make a lovely present.
Jo And I shall get the best slippers to be had!

Hannah enters from the hall bearing a tray laden with tea things. She is a middle-aged to elderly woman who has been with the family since Meg was born, and is considered by them all more as a friend than a servant. Her rather abrupt manner and dry humour do not entirely conceal a warm and loyal affection for her adopted family

Hannah (*setting her tray down on the table*) Land sakes! What's going on here? You girls are making a rare old noise and no mistake!
Amy We're planning Christmas surprises for Marmee.
Hannah Well, I reckon she'll need some peace and quiet when she gets home. She's been helping pack Christmas boxes for the soldiers all day—couldn't even come home to dinner—and, as if that weren't enough, she said she had a mind to call on that poor Hummel family on her way back. I guess they're in need again, and your Ma will help them. There never was such a woman for giving away vittles and clothes and things—no matter how little she has for herself.
Beth Poor Mrs Hummel. Her husband's just died, and she has six children and a new baby to look after.
Hannah Well, they've a guardian angel in your Ma. She'll not be long now; as soon as I hear her come in I shall make the tea, and you see that she drinks a good strong cupful while it's nice and hot. She'll be tired, and it's mortal cold outside. (*Turning to go*) Oh, I'd forgotten all about this. (*She produces an envelope from under her apron*) It came by hand this afternoon. (*To Meg*) It's for you, Miss Meg.
Meg Whoever can it be from?
Hannah If you really want to find out, I reckon the easiest thing to do is to open it.

Meg (*opening it*) Oh, what fun! It's a note of invitation from Mrs Gardiner! Just listen to this—"Mrs Gardiner would be happy to see Miss March and Miss Josephine at a little party on New Year's Eve." Doesn't that sound grand? Do you think Marmee will let us go?

Hannah I don't see any reason why not—you're young ladies now.

Jo winces

Well, I must get back to my kitchen. Now, don't let this fancy invite make you forget your Ma's toast.

Hannah exits

Beth takes up the toasting fork and bread from the tray, and settles by the fire

Meg Oh, Jo! Isn't it wonderful! It's ages since we went to a party! Now what shall we wear?

Jo What's the use of asking that, when you know we shall wear our poplins because we haven't anything else?

Amy (*somewhat piqued that the invitation did not include her*) Oh, bother the Gardiners and their wretched party. We must decide what to do about Marmee's presents, and she'll be here at any moment.

Beth We must let her think that we are getting things for ourselves and then we can surprise her.

Amy We'd better go shopping tomorrow afternoon for there won't be any other time, and we still need to rehearse for our play on Christmas night.

Jo Yes, and it has to be extra specially good this year. Marmee always enjoys our Christmas plays, and, with Father away, she needs cheering up as much as possible.

Meg I don't think I shall act in any more after this one. I'm getting too old for such things.

Jo Oh, fiddlesticks, Meg! You won't stop as long as you can trail round in a long white gown with your hair down, and wear gold paper jewellery. Besides you're the best actress we've got and there'll be an end of everything if you quit the boards. (*Becoming more practical*) We could rehearse a bit now. Come on, Amy, let's do the fainting scene. You are as stiff as a poker in that.

Amy I can't help it; I never saw anyone faint in the whole of my entire life—and I don't choose to make myself all black and blue tumbling flat as you do. If I can go down easily, I'll drop; if I can't, I shall fall into a chair and be graceful—and I don't care if Hugo does come at me with a pistol in that scene.

Jo Look, do it this way. Clasp your hands so, and stagger across the stage crying frantically "Roderigo! Save me! Save me!" (*She demonstrates in highly melodramatic manner, completing her performance with a harrowing scream*)

After a moment or two of uncertainty Amy endeavours to follow her example, but her movements are stiff and jerky, her delivery matter of fact and her final scream a little more than a loud "Ow!"

Jo (*hiding her face and groaning in despair*) It's no use! Oh, well, do the best you can when the time comes, and if the audience laugh don't blame me.

Beth (*endeavouring to pour oil on troubled waters*) I don't see how you can write and act such splendid things, Jo. You're a regular Shakespeare!

Jo Not quite, but I do think that my effort this year, *The Witches' Curse, An Operatic Tragedy* is my best yet. What I should really like to try is *Macbeth*—if only we had a trap-door for Banquo. I've always wanted to do the killing part. "Is that a dagger I see before me?" (*She adopts an exaggerated pose of highly theatrical terror "rolling her eyes and clutching at the air, as she had seen a famous tragedian do"*)

As she lurches about the room, Beth rises from the fireplace to confront her with the toasting fork

Beth No, it's a toasting fork! (*She advances on Jo, forcing her back into the sofa amid laughter and loud applause from the others*)

At this moment, the sound of her arrival lost in the noise, Marmee appears in the archway still wearing her cloak and bonnet. She is tired after a hard day and a long, cold walk home, but her nature is a warm and sympathetic one. Despite her fatigue, the uproar does not distress her; her eyes twinkle, and she smiles in pleasure at the scene before her. To the girls she is simply "the most splendid mother in the world"

Marmee (*as the noise subsides*) Well, girls, I am glad to find you so merry!

The girls turn and greet their mother loudly and affectionately. Jo flings her arms about her and hugs her. Meg takes her bonnet and cloak. Amy follows Jo's example. Beth puts the final touches to the chair by the fire while she waits to greet her mother there

Jo Marmee! How are you? (*She calls*) Hannah, Marmee's home! Time for the tea.

Meg Mother, we were beginning to wonder what had happened to you.

Beth Come and sit down, Marmee, you must be tired.

Amy Hannah says you are to have your tea good and hot.

Marmee is helped out of her cloak and bonnet and into her slippers

Marmee Thank you, my dears. How have you got on today? Is your cold better, Meg? Jo, you look tired out. Has anyone called, Beth? How was school today, Amy?

The girls answer her queries as Jo makes up the fire. Meg busies herself with the tea things. Beth brings a footstool. Amy holds on firmly to her mother's hand

Hannah reappears with the teapot

Marmee settles thankfully into the chair by the fire

My, it's been a busy day; there was so much to do getting the Christmas boxes ready to go tomorrow.

Meg Hannah said you were calling on poor Mrs Hummel on your way home.

Marmee Yes, I took them firewood and a basket of food. They are in a desperate plight.

Beth How is the new baby, Marmee?

Marmee Very thin and undernourished like all the children. They have no fire and they are all huddled into one bed to keep warm.

Meg Mother, how dreadful!

Marmee That's not all. Mrs Hummel has been so poorly since the new baby came that she has been unable to work, and until I got there they had literally nothing to eat. (*She pauses, looking around at all four faces*) My girls, I wonder, shall we give them some of the good things we have put by for our Christmas so that theirs may be a little happier?

Girls Yes, oh, yes! Let's do what we can to help them.

Marmee I thought you would want to help. Tomorrow we will all go around together and deliver our gifts. Bless you! Now, as a reward for your goodness of heart, what do you think a soldier home on leave brought me today?

Slight pause

Jo A letter! A letter from Father!

Meg Oh, Mother, really?

Amy What does he say, Marmee, please tell us!

Beth How is he? Is he well?

Marmee Yes, a letter—a nice long letter. He is well and sends all sorts of loving wishes for Christmas and an especial message for you girls. (*Looking through the letter*) Yes, here it is; he says: "Give them all my dear love and a kiss. Tell them I think of them by day, pray for them by night, and find my best comfort in their affection at all times. A year seems very long to wait before I see them, but remind them that while we wait we may all work, so that these hard days need not be wasted. I know they will remember all I said to them, that they will be loving children to you, will do their duty faithfully and conduct themselves so beautifully, that when I come back to them I may be fonder and prouder than ever of my little women."

There is a silence during which Marmee folds up the letter, and hands feel for handkerchiefs. Suddenly Hannah, who has listened entranced and fought her emotion unsuccessfully, throws her apron over her face and sobs

Hannah Oh, the dear, good man!

Hannah exits hurriedly to the kitchen

Marmee Poor Hannah. She has been with us for so long now that she misses your father as much as the rest of us.

Meg pulls herself together and turns her attention to the teapot

Meg Oh, Marmee, we've forgotten all about your tea. (*She pours*) I think it was so splendid of Father to go as a chaplain when he was too old to be drafted and not strong enough to be a soldier.

Jo I wish *I* could go as a drummer or a nurse, so I could be near him and help him.

Amy It must be very disagreeable to sleep in a tent, and eat all sorts of bad tasting things, and drink out of a tin mug.

Beth When will he come home, Marmee?

Marmee Not for many months, I'm afraid, dear. He will stay and do his work faithfully as long as he can, and we won't ask for him back a minute sooner than he can be spared. (*Brightening*) Jo dear, draw the curtains and let us make ourselves cosy for the evening. There is some sewing to do and, perhaps, you will read aloud to us as we work, eh?

Jo (*at the window*) Oh, look! The lamps are lit in the drawing-room of the big house next door, and they haven't drawn the curtains. I can see right in!

Meg Jo, you shouldn't do that; it's like eavesdropping.

Jo (*unheeding this rebuke*) There's old Mr Laurence sitting in a great chair and the Laurence boy playing to him on the most beautiful grand piano. It's simply enormous—oh, Beth, do come and see it, it will make you quite green . . .

Marmee (*before Beth can move*) Certainly not! Jo, draw the curtains at once and come away from the window. What would Mr Laurence and his grandson think if they saw you peering over at them?

Jo (*turning into the room, but without drawing the curtains*) But, Marmee, it isn't as if they are complete strangers to us. You told us once that old Mr Laurence knew your father years ago, and I have spoken to the Laurence boy.

Amy (*scandalized*) Without a formal introduction?

Jo Oh, don't be so stuffy, Amy. It was when one of Beth's kittens ran over into their garden and he brought it back.

Beth He seems very nice, and he looks as if he'd like to know us, but he's bashful.

Jo I think he is a capital fellow, and I mean to get to know him for he needs friends. I am sure he does.

Marmee I have no objection to your knowing him if a proper opportunity occurs. But Mr Laurence keeps very much to himself, and I wouldn't wish to presume on a very slight acquaintance.

Meg Why does he do that, Mother?

Marmee I believe he has had some very great tragedy in his family which has made him disinclined to mix with other people, and that, of course, makes it difficult for his grandson to get to know anyone.

Jo He keeps the boy shut up, when he isn't riding or walking with his tutor, and makes him study very hard.

Meg The Moffats told me that they asked him to their party, but he didn't go.

Jo Well, I think it's jolly hard luck and . . .

Marmee Now, that will do! It is not for us to criticize and know better. Please draw the curtains and come to the fire.

Jo (*at the window*) Oh, they've gone now! (*As she starts to draw the curtains she is arrested by something else, and abruptly pauses*) Christopher Columbus! It's ... (*peering out, unable to believe her eyes*) ... it's ... yes, it is! (*She turns back into the room*) It's Aunt March! Oh, Marmee, Aunt March's carriage is drawing up outside ...!

Everyone is astounded! There are general cries of "Aunt March?", "Here?", "Never!", "Coming here?", "But she never calls on us", etc.

Marmee (*rising*) Whatever can she want? I don't think she has called on us in ten years. Jo, did she say anything to you about calling this evening?

Jo No, Marmee, I can't understand it.

Marmee Well, she's here now. Quick, girls, let's make the room tidy. Meg, take the tray back to the kitchen and ask Hannah to make some fresh tea. Beth, Amy, I think you had better go upstairs and wait there until I send for you. Jo, you stay here in case Aunt March wishes to speak to you.

The front door bell rings loudly and autocratically

There she is!

Meg, Beth and Amy exit quickly

You let her in, Jo; Hannah is busy and, anyway, I think Aunt March rather terrifies her!

Jo goes out to the front door

Marmee positions herself in front of the fire bracing herself for something of an ordeal

A moment later Aunt March enters and pauses in the archway surveying the room. She is a formidable, autocratic old lady, richly dressed, and walking with a cane. She has a slight limp

Aunt March (*before Marmee has time to greet her*) Well, niece, aren't you going to ask me to sit down?

Marmee Good evening, Aunt March, do come in and make yourself at home. May I take your cloak?

Aunt March moves to the sofa

Jo enters

Aunt March (*sitting*) No, thank you, don't intend to stay that long. Just thought I'd come around and see how you and the girls were—can never get any information out of Josephine here. (*She pronounces this "Josyphine"—much to Jo's disgust*)

Marmee We are all well, I am glad to say. Meg has had a slight cold ...

Aunt March Cold? Not surprised, the way young people go on these days it's a wonder they don't all die of pneumonia.

Marmee And are you keeping well, Aunt March?

Aunt March (*affronted by such an enquiry*) Me? Well? I am never well! My old trouble here (*patting her leg*) gives me constant pain, and, of course, I get so little sleep.

Marmee But Jo tells me that you always sleep soundly for an hour or so every day after dinner.

Aunt March (*annoyed at being caught out*) Nonsense! I am only resting my eyes from the light while she reads to me. I have never really slept for over thirty years—I just lose myself for a little while, that's all.

Jo (*with studied innocence*) But you never find yourself again very soon, do you, Aunt?

Marmee Jo, don't be impertinent. It must be very trying for you, Aunt March.

Aunt March (*after a baleful glare at Jo*) How's that husband of yours? My nephew?

Marmee He is well, thank you, and seems to find the rigours of camp life not too difficult to bear.

Aunt March Beyond me what he wanted to go gallivanting off to the war for at all at his age. Why couldn't he stay at home and be a chaplain?

Marmee (*quietly*) He did what he knew to be the right thing, and, though I miss him dearly, I would not have it otherwise. The men need him, and he feels that he is doing good work among them.

Aunt March That's questionable! Can't say that his judgement is always unerring. Look how he lost all his money helping that good-for-nothing friend of his a few years ago. I told him, I said to him at the time . . .

Marmee Aunt March. Whatever my husband did he did as a Christian gentleman to help a dear friend in misfortune; that everything was lost in the transaction is no reflection on either of them. I am sorry, but I cannot sit here in his own house and hear you speak ill of him when . . .

Aunt March Highty-tighty, then! Highty-tighty! Didn't I do what I could to help? Didn't I offer to adopt one of the girls and bring her up?

Marmee We told you then that we couldn't give up one of our girls, not for a fortune. Rich or poor we will keep together and be happy in one another.

Aunt March Mighty independent, I must say. Well, you know your own business best, I suppose. Though it seems a pity that you didn't take up my offer.

Marmee We are, of course, most grateful to you for having Jo as a help and companion.

Aunt March Wouldn't have her if she didn't suit me! I took a fancy to her and I am always right in these matters. She does well enough—though I think sometimes that she takes more interest in her late Uncle March's library than in attending to my wants.

Jo Oh, but Aunt March, I . . .

Aunt March That is enough, Miss! You know as well as I do that you spend every spare minute you can find in among those books.

Marmee I am afraid that Jo has a great weakness for reading, but she should not neglect her duties to indulge her pleasures.

Aunt March Oh! Her duties! They are light enough in all conscience—wind yarn, wash the poodle, feed Polly, my sweet parrot, fetch and carry, and read aloud *Belsham's Essays* (*with a look at Jo*) of which *I*, at least, never tire.

Marmee Am I to understand then, Aunt March, that you are here this evening to complain of Jo's behaviour?

Aunt March (*astounded*) Complain! Complain? Whatever gave you the idea that I would ever complain about anything?

Marmee (*at a loss*) Oh, I see—then may I ask the reason for your visit?

Aunt March Reason! Mercy on us! That should be plain enough, I should think! Why should an invalid like myself, racked with pain, turn out on a cold winter's night? For no reason other than to wish you a happy Christmas, of course, what else?

Marmee I—oh—er—thank you, Aunt March, I . . .

Aunt March (*cutting in*) And with my nephew away playing at soldiers, I have no doubt that things will not be so plentiful here at home this year. Josephine, run to the carriage, girl, and fetch the parcels from the coachman.

Jo exits UL

(*Turning to Marmee*) Nothing much, you know, just a small gift for each girl—a trifle of lace, a little brooch, some ribbons, and so on. Oh, yes, and there is a basket with a ham and butter and cakes and things. Good, wholesome produce—I do not think rich food is good for young people. At any rate, it will keep all of you from starving.

Jo reappears laden with a basket of food, and a number of packages

Ah! Put them down, girl, before you drop them! (*She turns to go*) Now, I must go, there are a great many things requiring my attention, and I have not the time to stay here listening to your gossip. (*She pauses at the archway*) And, remember—none of the parcels may be opened until Christmas morning!

With a brisk tug at her gloves Aunt March exits before either Marmee or Jo can reply

For a moment they are speechless with surprise

Jo Marmee!

Marmee (*amid mutual laughter*) Well, Jo, I really don't know what to say, and to think that after we refused to let her adopt one of you, she wouldn't speak to us for a whole year!

Jo After Christmas I'll be extra good, I promise, and do all she asks me with a smile—even to reading the boring . . . I mean, *brilliant* essays of Mr Belsham!

Marmee Now, you run upstairs, dear, and tell the others that the ordeal is over and I'll pack all these good things away (*imitating Aunt March*) "for Christmas morning"!

Jo Marmee, may we have some time to rehearse our play upstairs, please? There is still quite a lot to do for it.

Marmee Why, yes, of course, I have several things to do down here and will call you when I am done—but, Jo dear, try not to make too much noise!

Jo All right, Marmee!

Jo exits noisily upstairs

*Marmee sorts the gifts, reading the messages on them and smiling to herself.
These she puts on one side, then gathers up the basket and begins to move
towards the kitchen*

The front door bell rings

She pauses momentarily in surprise

Hannah appears on her way to answer it

Marmee moves up to the archway, speaking as she goes

Marmee It's all right, Hannah, I'll go. Would you take these things, please?
They are Christmas presents from Aunt March!

Hannah Christmas presents from your Aunt March! Land sakes! That'll
make the angels sing!

Hannah exits as Marmee goes to the front door

Voices are heard off L

*Marmee enters, followed by Laurie. He is a tall young man with dark, good
looks which betray his part-Italian blood. Normally lively and confident, at
the moment he is a little nervous and hesitant in unfamiliar company. He is
carrying a bunch of beautiful, hothouse flowers and two bottles of wine
wrapped in tissue paper*

Marmee Do please come in, Mr Laurence, it is nice of you to call.

Laurie Thank you, Mrs March, I am really here on behalf of my grandfather. He asked me to present his compliments and his apologies.

Marmee His apologies?

Laurie Yes, he asked me to say (*thinking hard as he strives to remember
exactly what his grandfather has told him to say*) that he feels he has been
very remiss in not calling to pay his respects to you, the daughter of his
old friend, but he hopes that you will forgive the tardiness of an old man
who ventures but rarely into society.

Marmee How very kind of him. Please sit down.

*Laurie is about to do so when he suddenly remembers that there is something
more of his grandfather's message*

Laurie And he hopes that you will do him the honour of accepting these
two bottles of Madeira with the compliments of the season.

Marmee (*taking the bottles*) Thank you. (*With a smile*) Dear me, you did
have to learn a long speech, didn't you?

Laurie (*relaxing with a laugh*) Yes, it was rather—I was afraid I should
forget half of it—oh, and these flowers are from me. I picked them myself
in the conservatory.

Marmee How very sweet of you! They are lovely! Please thank your
grandfather most warmly for me. Perhaps you would both like to come

and take tea with us one day and meet my family? (*She puts the gifts on the table above the sofa*)

Laurie I should like that very much indeed, Mrs March.

Marmee (*sitting*) I believe that you have met my daughter, Jo, already?

Laurie (*sitting*) Yes, when the kitten ran into our garden. She is full of life, isn't she? She told me that she wants to be an authoress.

Marmee Oh, yes, our Jo is very lively and she is always busy scribbling away up in a little study she has made for herself in the attic.

Laurie Meg is the pretty one, isn't she, and Beth the rosy one who stays at home a good deal; and the curly-haired one who sketches and paints is Amy, I believe?

Marmee (*laughing*) For someone who has never really met my girls, you seem to know a great deal about them! Pray how did you discover all that?

Laurie (*feeling that perhaps he has said too much*) Why, you see, I often hear them calling to one another, and when I am alone at home I can't help looking over here at your house; you seem always to be having such good times. Sometimes you don't draw the curtains, and when the lamps are lighted it's like a picture to look in and see you all at table or busy with some household task, I am afraid that I can't help watching.

Marmee Do you live alone with your grandfather?

Laurie Yes, my parents are both dead. Grandpa lives among his books and doesn't take much interest in what happens outside. Mr Brooke, my tutor, only comes in during the day so I am rather much alone at times. That's why I am afraid I have taken to watching all your comings and goings.

Marmee Well, when you have met my girls there will be no need for you to watch any more for you must come over whenever you are lonely and join in our simple amusements. I know the girls will make you very welcome.

Laurie (*rising*) Thank you very much, Mrs March, it's good of you to receive me so kindly. I will give your message to Grandpa and tell him . . .

This speech is interrupted by a crash from upstairs, followed by the classic line "Roderigo! Save me! Save me!" and a loud scream—Amy has evidently improved

Marmee Oh dear, you must excuse the noise. Jo is rehearsing the others in a family play for Christmas—and I am afraid things are inclined to get a bit out of hand at times. (*She rings the bell for Hannah*) That is why I can't introduce you to them now—I have no idea what state of uproar they are in!

There is another crash from upstairs

Jo (*off*) Alas! Alas for Zara!

Noises of general confusion

Laurie (*with a smile*) Yes, I see what you mean.

   Hannah enters

Marmee Will you show Mr Laurence out, Hannah? (*She shakes his hand*)

Good-night, Mr Laurence, and thank you for the lovely flowers. We shall look forward to your visiting us again quite soon.

Laurie Good-night, Mrs March, I shall look forward to coming.

For a moment Laurie looks wistfully upstairs then exits with Hannah

Marmee puts the wine away in the cupboard and smells the flowers

Hannah returns

Hannah What a nice young gentleman! But, if all I hear is true, he's left a sight too much on his own.

Marmee Yes, I'm sure he doesn't get much fun over in that big house all by himself. He needs some lively company.

Sound of a louder crash followed by a jumble of voices and laughter in which Jo dominates with . . .

Jo (*off*) What ho, minion! I have need of thee! Come, Zara, we must away!

Hannah Seems to me there's a whole lot of lively company right here on his doorstep!

Marmee (*smiling*) And I have a feeling that we shall be seeing quite a lot more of that young man in the near future!

Marmee and Hannah laugh quietly together as they exit

The Lights fade slowly to Black-out

SCENE 2

The same. Early evening on New Year's Eve

As the Lights rise there is an atmosphere of excitement as the two younger girls help their sisters to get ready for the Gardiners' party. Beth is busily fastening the final hooks on Meg's dress. Meg, standing before the fire, has half a dozen curls in curling papers on her forehead and looks harassed

Meg (*smoothing her hand over her dress*) If only I had a new dress for the party! The Gardiners are such an elegant family and their guests are always so fashionable. Mother says that I may have a silk dress for my birthday, but that is an everlasting time to wait!

Beth I'm sure this dress looks like silk, Meg; it's really as good as new, and you look awfully nice in it.

Amy enters down the stairs

Amy There's the lace handkerchief that I said you might borrow, but do be careful with it for it's the very bestest one I have.

Meg (*turning to take the handkerchief*) Thank you, Amy.

Amy (*seeing the curling papers*) You're not going to the party like that, are you?

Meg No, of course not, Jo's going to pinch the curls in with hot tongs for me in a moment. Curls on the forehead are all the fashion this season you know.

Amy (*impressed*) Oh, Beth, won't it be wonderful when we are old enough to go to evening parties too?

Meg Where is Jo? It's past seven o'clock already and the last time I saw her she had not even started to dress. I don't believe she likes parties very much.

Beth She says she hates being all dressed up and on her best behaviour. She'd much rather settle down with a book and a bag of apples up in her attic.

Meg Be a dear, Amy, run up and see how she is getting on. It would never do for us to be late. There, Beth, how do I look?

Amy exits shouting for Jo

Beth (*with pride*) A real belle!

Meg This new ribbon sets it off nicely, and Marmee's pearl brooch gives the bodice a very aristocratic air—she is a dear to lend it to me. (*She raises the hem of her dress*) And don't my new slippers look lovely?

Beth Yes, but are they comfortable?

Meg They pinch a little when I walk (*she winces slightly as she tests them*), but I expect that will soon wear off. Anyway, I haven't any others that go so well with this dress.

Amy enters

Amy (*as she returns*) Jo's coming. And I've brought the curling-tongs. (*She moves to the fire and puts the tongs by it to heat*)

Meg Oh, good! Pinching the curls into place won't take a moment and then I shall feel the very height of fashion!

Amy You look really elegant, Meg, I am sure that none of the other girls will look any more fine than you.

Meg Oh, I am so glad you think ...

Their enthusiastic chatter is arrested by the arrival of Jo who, although she is wearing her party dress and has made an effort to groom herself for the ordeal, still has a rather casual, slap-dash air about her

Jo (*preparing for the wrath to come*) Meg, it's so long since I put this dress on that I'd completely forgotten all about the burn at the back. (*She turns revealing a large scorch mark on the skirt*) Whatever shall I do? It shows badly and I can't get any of it out.

Meg (*her pleasure suddenly clouded*) Oh, Jo! Why will you stand in front of the fire like a man! That's not the first dress you've scorched and spoilt by doing so. Well, you've nothing else to wear, so you'll have to wear that, I suppose—though what the Gardiners will think I just don't know.

Jo I shall just have to sit still all I can and keep my back out of sight. (*Brightly*) The front is all right anyway!

Meg Where are your gloves, Jo?

Jo (*somewhat shamefacedly*) I'm afraid they're stained with the lemonade I got on them at the last party we went to—I couldn't ask Marmee for new ones, they are so expensive, so I shall just go without.

Meg Oh, really Jo! You are the most provoking girl! You must have gloves! Gloves are more important than anything else.

Amy (*who shares with Meg a strong sense of what is "correct"*) Meg's right. A real lady is always known by her neat boots, her gloves, and her handkerchief.

Meg Of course, you must have them! If you don't, then I won't go! I would be so mortified if you went without them.

Jo (*flopping into a chair*) Then I'll stay where I am!

Beth (*ever the peacemaker*) Oh, you mustn't spoil the evening like that. Can't you make your gloves do even if they are soiled?

Jo (*grudgingly*) I suppose I could hold them crumpled up in my hand, so no one knows how stained they are. (*A bright idea occurs to her*) No, I'll tell you how we can manage! We'll each wear one good one and carry one bad one.

Meg (*dubiously*) Your hands are bigger than mine, and you will stretch my glove dreadfully . . .

Jo (*losing patience*) Then I'll go without, and I don't care what people say!

Meg Oh, you may have it, you may! Only please don't stain it! (*They exchange gloves*) And you will behave nicely won't you? You won't stare or say "Christopher Columbus" at the top of your voice?

Jo Oh, Meg! It's only a party at Mrs Gardiner's, we're not going to meet President Lincoln! (*She moves to the fire to pick up the tongs with the aid of the kettle-holder which hangs beside it*) Now, let's get your curls done.

Meg seats herself as Jo moves back to her

Don't you worry about me. I'll be as prim as I can, and not get into any scrapes if I can help it. (*As she works on Meg's curls*) But if I forget, and you see me doing anything wrong, just remind me by a wink, will you?

Meg I shall do nothing of the sort. Winking is not at all ladylike. I shall lift my eyebrows if anything is wrong and nod if you're all right. Now, when we get there, Jo, do hold your shoulders straight, and take short steps, and don't shake hands if you are introduced . . . (*Suddenly, she sniffs anxiously*) Ought they to smoke like that?

Jo (*confidently*) It's the dampness drying, that's all.

Amy What a queer smell! It's like burnt feathers.

Beth (*a little uncertainly*) I expect it's the scorched paper.

Jo (*laying down the tongs, with the air of a great artist*) There, now I will take off the papers and you will see a cloud of little ringlets.

Handing Meg a hand mirror, Jo removes the papers briskly and, with each, the curl comes away also. Jo stands with a handful of curls; Meg sits with a bare forehead

Meg (*peering into the mirror, scarcely able to believe her eyes*) Oh! Oh! Oh! What have you done? I'm spoilt! I can't go! My hair, oh my hair!

There is general consternation

Marmee enters

Marmee Well, girls, are you ready? It is getting late.

Meg Oh, Mother, look at my hair! It's ruined! I can't go like this. Oh, Jo, how could you?

Jo I'm sorry, Meg, I am really. The tongs must have been too hot. Just my luck; you shouldn't have asked me to do it. I always spoil everything. Oh dear, what a blunderbuss I am!

Meg (*in tears*) It serves me right for trying to be too fine. Oh I wish I'd let my hair alone.

Marmee inspects the damage

Beth What a shame! It was so smooth and pretty.

Marmee (*thinking fast*) Now, dry your eyes. It's not so bad as you think. Pass me that comb, Amy, please. There, now, if we comb these strands forward into a fringe it will look quite neat and tidy, and when you get to the Gardiners' refasten your bow a little further forward on to the forehead and nothing will seem amiss.

Amy Marmee's right, and it will look quite fashionable too; I've seen many girls do it so.

Meg Oh, thank you so much. (*She kisses Marmee*) What should we do without you?

Marmee (*with a hug*) Help one another even more than you do now, I expect. Now, let me see these two fine young ladies of fashion!

Meg, recapturing her good spirits, rises and turns about for her mother's inspection Jo starts to follow her example, remembers her scorch mark, and presents only her front view

Yes, I think you will do very nicely! Now, into your cloaks and away to enjoy yourselves before there are any more disasters!

Beth and Amy help with the cloaks and the party moves towards the archway

Don't eat too much supper, and come away at eleven when I send Hannah for you. Give my kind regards to Mrs Gardiner and her girls!

With much chattering the younger girls take Meg and Jo to the front door leaving Marmee in the archway

Have a good time, my dears—oh, have you both got nice pocket handkerchiefs?

Jo ⎫ (*off, together*) ⎰ Yes, thank you, Marmee; Goodbye.
Meg ⎭   ⎱ Goodbye Mother, goodbye Amy, Beth. *ad lib*

Marmee begins to tidy the room, collecting the mirror, tongs, comb etc

Amy and Beth return

Amy Oh, I wish I were going as well, I do envy them.

Marmee Never mind, dear, your turn will come, and then you will be going to lots of parties. (*Pausing reflectively*) I hope they enjoy themselves this evening; I'm afraid those high-heeled slippers of Meg's are too tight for real comfort, but she is too delighted with them to admit it. (*Completing her task*) Take these things upstairs, please, and then I think you had better get ready for bed.

They start to go somewhat forlornly. Their wistful faces catch Marmee's eye

Oh, my dears, don't look so forlorn! There's a little consolation treat for you upstairs. I've made some of your favourite cookies, and put them up there for you with some fresh milk.

Beth   (*together*)   Oh, Marmee, that is kind! Thank you so much!
Amy   How lovely, Marmee! Thank you!

Brightening appreciably at this pleasant prospect, Beth and Amy hasten upstairs as ...

Marmee moves to the fire

The Lights fade and remain lowered for a few moments to denote the passage of about two and a half hours

When the Lights come up Marmee is reading in her chair by the fire with a small woollen shawl around her shoulders

The clock strikes ten

Marmee looks up and then settles herself again and continues reading for a few moments. All is quiet, then ...

A carriage is heard approaching and stopping outside; a moment later the front door opens noisily and ...

Jo bursts into the room

Marmee (*in surprise*) Jo! Why are you home so early? Hannah wasn't coming for you for another hour.
Jo (*her words tumbling out in a torrent of excitement mixed with reassurance*) It's nothing to worry about, Marmee, so don't get into a fret! Meg turned her ankle while she was dancing—I think that it was those new slippers that did it—and then Laurie suggested that ...
Marmee (*trying to keep up with the garbled flow of words*) Laurie?
Jo Young Mr Laurence! He was at the party with his tutor, Mr Brooke, and he said he would bring us home in his carriage. Wasn't that splendid of him?
Marmee (*endeavouring to get a word in*) Well, where are they now, Jo?
Jo Outside helping Meg out of the carriage. I came on ahead to tell you what had happened.
Marmee Go and ask them to come in, my dear.

Jo needs no second bidding and goes out as quickly as she came in

Marmee arranges the cushions on the sofa

Meg enters, supported on either side by Laurie and John Brooke and with Jo bringing up the rear. Brooke is a tall, fair, handsome young man in his mid-twenties

Good evening, Mr Laurence, it is kind of you to help in this way. Come, Meg, dear, over to the sofa where you may rest your foot, and then we'll see what damage has been done.

The others help Meg to the sofa

There, that's better.

Laurie May I introduce my tutor and friend Mr John Brooke? (*To Brooke*) Mrs March.

Marmee How do you do Mr Brooke? I am afraid that this little catastrophe has rather cut short the evening for you and Mr Laurence.

Brooke Not at all, Mrs March, we usually leave early, don't we, Laurie? Mr Laurence doesn't like his grandson out too late.

Marmee removes Meg's shoe and examines her foot and ankle

Laurie Besides it is raining hard and Miss Meg would have been soaked if she had had to limp all the way home.

Brooke Has there been much damage done, Ma'am?

Marmee No, I do not think that there are any bones broken, thank goodness; it is just a nasty sprain. You'll have to rest up for a few days, Meg.

Laurie Oh, that's a relief! We were afraid it might be more serious, weren't we, Miss Jo?

Jo (*who has been aware of the formality in Laurie's manner in the presence of her mother*) Christopher Columbus! Why are we so formal all of a sudden? We were getting on so well at the party and it was "Laurie" "Meg" and "Jo" then!

Meg tries to signal her disapproval to Jo by raising her eyebrows

Oh, it's no use raising your eyebrows at me like that, Meg. I said I'd be on my best behaviour at the Gardiners—but I'm home now, and have had quite enough prudence and propriety for one evening!

Marmee (*with a smile*) You mustn't be too shocked by Jo, she is a firm believer in speaking her own mind—especially in her own home. But you must feel at home here too, and Jo won't let you stand on ceremony for long!

Laurie Thank you, Mrs March; I wish you'd call me Laurie too.

Marmee Why, of course, I will! Now, this ankle must have a cold compress without further delay. Jo, while I go and get things for it, will you give our guests a glass of Madeira. Please sit down and make yourselves comfortable.

Marmee exits to the kitchen

Jo busies herself getting the wine

Brooke This is very hospitable of your mother, but I am afraid that we intrude.

Meg Not at all, Mr Brooke, Mother likes company, and it would be inhospitable to let you go without some refreshment after the kind way in which you have helped us this evening.

Jo (*passing the glasses around*) Besides, we are neighbours, and you needn't think you'd be a bother. We *want* to get to know you and I've been trying to do it this ever so long!

There is a good-natured laugh from everyone as John Brooke raises his glass to Meg

Brooke To your speedy recovery, Miss March!

Meg Thank you, Mr Brooke, my ankle feels easier already.

Jo (*brushing aside such pleasantries*) Now, tell me, are you really called Laurie Laurence? It's an odd mouthful of a name.

Laurie (*laughing*) No, my first name is Theodore, but I don't like it for the fellows called me Dora—so I made them call me Laurie instead.

Jo I hate my name too. Josephine is so sentimental! I wish everyone would call me Jo instead. My Aunt March, who I am with every day, *will* call me "Josy-Phine". Tell me, how did you stop the boys calling you Dora?

Laurie I thrashed 'em.

Jo (*reflectively and with some disappointment*) Well, I suppose I can't very well thrash Aunt March so I shall have to bear it.

Laurie (*catching sight of a picture on the mantelpiece*) Is this your father?

Jo Yes, that's father. Oh, we do miss him so much, he's so far away and . . .

As they turn to examine the picture, talking quietly to each other, Meg and Brooke, who have been listening in quiet amusement, pick up a conversation of their own

Meg Is Laurie always a good pupil, Mr Brooke?

Brooke (*with a smile*) Perhaps not always, Miss March, for he does not always apply himself as he should, but it is very rewarding when he does, and one begins to see the fruit of one's work.

Meg I teach, also, but I must confess that I don't really enjoy it. I only wish that I liked it as much as you obviously do.

Brooke I think you would if you had Laurie as a pupil. He is particularly good at languages. His French is quite fluent and we are now working hard at his German. In a few months, I think . . .

Meg (*interrupting*) German! You are teaching him German?

Brooke Why, yes, do you speak it?

Meg No—that is, my father was teaching me before he went away, and although I try to practise myself I am afraid I don't get on very fast alone, for I have no-one to correct my pronunciation.

Brooke Then, perhaps, you will allow me . . .?

Meg (*confused*) Oh, no, I . . . I couldn't bother you to . . . I . . . I didn't mean that when I said . . .

Brooke (*with a smile*) No, of course not, I quite understand; but, if you will allow me, I will have a word with your mother and see what can be arranged.

Meg That is very kind of you, Mr Brooke, I . . .

Brooke Not at all, it would give me great pleasure to be of some assistance.

Something in the way Brooke looks at Meg makes her change the subject rather abruptly

Meg You are very happy with Laurie and old Mr Laurence?

Brooke Indeed, yes; I shall be very sorry to leave them when Laurie goes to college in a year or so.

Meg And what will become of you then?

Brooke (*without self-pity*) Well, I have no family now, and few friends, so I think if the war is still on I shall turn soldier.

Meg I am sure that Mr Laurence and Laurie will regret the parting as much as you do.

Brooke Mine will be the greater loss, I feel, for I am beginning to realize what a very charming neighbourhood this is. (*The look in his eyes is a steady one with no trace of boldness or flirtation*)

Before Meg can find breath for reply, Marmee enters with a small tray of bandages, lint, etc.

Marmee (*as she enters*) I have been longer than I expected. We've been looking everywhere for this bottle of arnica which is so good for sprains. For some reason best known to itself, it was in the larder among the jars of pickles! (*She sets down the tray*)

Brooke (*rising*) We must bid you good-night, Mrs March. You have much to do I am sure. Thank you again for your hospitality. Are you ready, Laurie?

Marmee Good-night, Mr Brooke; good-night, Laurie—we are looking forward to you and your grandfather taking tea with us tomorrow. I was so pleased when he replied to my note and said he would come. Thank you again for bringing Meg home, will you excuse me if I don't see you to the door? I must bind this ankle without any more delay. Jo will see you out.

Brooke and Laurie exit with Jo amid general "Good-nights" etc.

Marmee sets to work to bind the ankle as the front door closes behind the guests

But she is to be disturbed still further, for two figures in night attire appear on the stairs. Amy is aiding nature by wearing curl papers and has a peg on her nose

Amy Marmee, please may we come down and hear about the party?

Marmee Amy! Beth! I thought you were asleep hours ago.

Beth We were so excited we just lay awake talking, and then we heard the carriage arriving . . .

Amy . . . and we crept out onto the landing, but didn't dare to come down—though we heard everything.

Marmee You are very naughty, eavesdropping, and, Amy dear, do take that clothes peg off your nose.

Amy But, Marmee, you know that I always sleep with it on—to improve the shape of my nose—it really is my worst feature. (*She removes the peg*)

Jo returns

Jo (*rummaging in her evening-bag*) Here you are, pets, I brought you some bon-bons as a little treat.

Meg (*dismayed at this revelation*) Jo! You didn't take them from the supper table?

Jo Yes, I don't think anybody saw me.

Meg How can you be sure? What would the Gardiners think if they saw you? Or Laurie! Or Mr Brooke?

Jo Laurie would just laugh, and what has it to do with Mr Brooke?

Meg (*confused*) Well, he would consider us very ill-mannered young ladies and ...

Jo Oh, stuff!

Amy Tell us about the party, please! Tell about the party!

Jo We had a capital time. Meg danced nearly every dance, in spite of her shoes, until she hurt her ankle.

Beth Didn't you dance, Jo?

Jo Oh, I'm not so very fond of dancing and, anyway, I was trying to hide this burn on my skirt. I was sitting in a little alcove enjoying myself no end watching everyone else, when Laurie came up and asked if he might dance with me. He looked so disappointed and hurt when I refused, and, as I couldn't think of any other excuse on the spur of the moment, I told him the truth.

Meg (*shocked once more*) You told him about the burn?

Jo Yes, why not? He thought it was a great lark and laughed no end. So we sat and talked; and, then, just before supper Meg was dancing with a big, red-haired youth who ...

Meg His hair is *auburn*, not red, and he's a very polite, well-mannered young gentleman.

Jo He looked like a grasshopper in a fit. Laurie and I couldn't help laughing, didn't you hear us?

Meg No, thank goodness; it was very rude of you! (*Taking up the story*) It was then that I turned my ankle. Laurie and Mr Brooke came to my aid ...

Jo And I heard Mr Brooke call the *auburn*-haired gentleman a "careless fellow" for dancing too fast and not looking about him.

Meg (*with more than usual interest*) Did he? (*Pulling herself together*) Then we had supper during which Jo succeeded in spilling coffee all over her one good glove (*obviously, an incident that has bitten into Meg's soul*). And Laurie offered to drive us home.

Jo And home we came in a closed carriage feeling very festive and elegant.

Marmee (*laughing*) Well, my girls, I hope this taste of high life won't make you too discontented with your own lot.

Jo No, Marmee, I don't believe fine ladies enjoy themselves one bit more than we do. In spite of our burnt hair, old gowns, odd gloves, and tight slippers that sprain our ankles when we are silly enough to wear them.

Marmee (*rising, to Beth and Amy*) Now, off to bed at once you two—and no more getting up, please! I shall be up in a minute to tuck you in—once again!

Beth and Amy exit upstairs

Meg dear, let us try your weight on that ankle and see if it is any better with the binding.

Meg rises, supported by her mother—her mind obviously elsewhere

Meg Yes, that's much better Marmee.

They progress towards the door

He's got very handsome brown eyes, hasn't he, Jo?

Jo is busily occupied collecting up their cloaks, etc.

Jo (*matter of factly*) Laurie's eyes are blue.
Meg No, I meant Mr Brooke.

Marmee and Meg exit upstairs

Jo (*as the truth slowly breaks in upon her*) Christopher Columbus!

The Lights fade to Black-out

SCENE 3

The same. New Year's Day. Afternoon

Winter sunshine smiles wanly through the window

When the Lights come up Marmee is seated on the sofa, her dress brightened by a pretty, silk shawl

Standing in front of the fire is the tall, distinguished figure of Mr Laurence. His white hair and craggy, aristocratic features might, at first sight, suggest a rather austere and distant character, but, as we shall discover, these conceal a dry sense of humour and a kindliness which shows in many actions

Mr Laurence and Marmee both hold a teacup and saucer. On the table behind the sofa stands a large tray of tea things including dishes of homemade confectionery and "Hannah's fruit cake". The atmosphere is pleasant; the tea-party and reunion have obviously gone well

Marmee Another cup of tea, Mr Laurence?
Mr Laurence No, thank you, ma'am. I have had a pleasant sufficiency. What a delightful visit this has been! It was good of you to receive me.

Marmee rises to take his cup and saucer, and return it, with her own, to the tray

Marmee It has been a special pleasure for me to meet you again after so long a time. My father always spoke of you with great affection.

Mr Laurence Ah, we were close friends, and saw much of each other until fate sent us our different ways. Just fancy, I knew you as a little girl, and now you have four daughters of your own! (*There is a slight pause. His voice saddens a little*) You know, perhaps, that I had two children—and lost them both?

Marmee (*knowing only part of the story*) I believe that you have endured much heartache.

Mr Laurence My little daughter died of fever when she was about the age of your youngest girl, and I have never quite reconciled myself to that loss. But, as to my son ... (*He pauses again in a moment of reflection before continuing*) He was in his early twenties when he met a young, Italian lady. She was lovely and good and, in every way accomplished ... indeed, there was nothing against her, but an old man's prejudice. They fell deeply in love and wished to marry, but I had other plans for my son, and strongly opposed such an alliance. I should have known better, but stubborn pride would have its way. Within a month they were wed. (*Turning to Marmee with a rueful smile*) Does that surprise you very greatly, ma'am?

Marmee (*gently, returning the smile*) Not really.

Mr Laurence (*resuming his story*) My son had never been strong; (*he indicates his chest*) his lungs, you know. He needed a warmer climate, so they went to live in Italy. I declined to have anything to do with them ... even to see them before they left. I never had the chance to see either of them again. She, poor lady, died in giving birth to Laurie, and, two months later, my son was laid to rest beside her.

Marmee Oh, I am sorry; what a terrible loss for you.

Mr Laurence I realized, too late, just what I had lost. Pride is a great sin, ma'am. There was only one thing left for me to do. I fetched my grandson home from Italy, and have devoted what is left of my life to giving him the same upbringing and education that his father had.

There is a little pause before Marmee speaks again

Marmee I am sure that you have only the boy's welfare at heart, but, if you will forgive me, I do feel that he is too much by himself. He is young, Mr Laurence, and so full of life. He needs young society, a measure of amusement, and healthful exercise.

Mr Laurence I suspect that you are right, ma'am. If I am inclined to keep him too much to myself, and coddle him, it is only because I remember the loss of the others.

Marmee That is understandable; but he will study harder and grow stronger for a little recreation among young people of his own age.

Mr Laurence (*with a smile; his manner relaxing*) On your own head be it, Mrs March! For your young ladies are the nearest young company, and he has already declared that "the Marches are regular splendid girls". I shall send him to plague you whenever he tires of his studies.

Marmee (*smiling also*) I shall be very pleased to see him, and I am sure the girls will make him very welcome. Jo will be delighted, she finds it difficult enough to resign herself to being a girl, and is always deploring the lack of a brother. You saw how anxious she was to get through tea when Laurie was kind enough to suggest showing her the horses in your stable. I fear that her enthusiasms sometimes make her forgetful of her manners.

Mr Laurence Not at all, I like to see enthusiasm in young people. Besides, their running off to see the horses has enabled us to talk more freely about old times, and nothing bores the young more quickly than that! But where are your other daughters? I should like to meet them as well.

Marmee Beth and Amy have been having tea with Meg who is spending the day in bed. Her ankle is rather swollen after that little misadventure last evening, and I thought the rest would do it good.

Mr Laurence Quite so. I am glad that Laurie and Brooke were at hand to be of assistance.

Marmee (*rising*) If you would care to come up, Mr Laurence, I should like very much for you to meet them.

Mr Laurence rises and they move to the stairs

To be quite frank, Beth is very shy of meeting you. I think that is why they asked leave to take tea upstairs—for Amy declared that she, too, would rather not come down without the others.

Mr Laurence (*surprised*) Frightened of meeting me? Dear me, we must do something to set that right. Let me see, isn't Beth the one I hear playing the piano sometimes when I pass the house?

Marmee Yes, she plays quite well, really, but I am afraid that on that piano in her room not all the notes are true!

Marmee exits up the stairs

Mr Laurence pauses briefly, and considers her last remark before following her

They pass out of sight, and for a moment the stage is empty

The clock on the mantelpiece chimes the half-hour and, then, voices are heard in the hall

Jo and Laurie enter from the kitchen. Jo is wearing a cloak and a wide scarf draped around her head and over her shoulders. Laurie has a long scarf around his neck. They are full of happy exhilaration. It is obvious that an immediate friendship has developed between them, but it is a friendship based on mutual enthusiams rather than romantic attraction

Jo (*looking around the room*) Oh, the tea-party seems to be over. Your grandfather must have gone home; I expect we missed him by coming around the other way. (*She moves to the table, removing her scarf and cloak, and examines the remains of tea*) Oh, good! There's still some of Hannah's fruit cake left. I am ready for another piece after our walk. Would you like some?

Laurie hesitates

Oh, go on! Here, catch! (*She throws a piece of fruit cake to him*)

Laurie catches it deftly with a laugh. They flop onto chairs and munch happily

What an absolutely splendid stable your grandfather has! I don't know which horse I liked best.

Laurie Yes, they are rather fine, aren't they? Grandpa's first love has always been horses. He used to ride a very great deal when he was younger, but he only goes out in the carriage now.

Jo We enjoyed our drive home last night and thought ourselves very elegant. Oh, that reminds me! Did you happened to find a glove in the carriage? In all the excitement Meg dropped one of hers, and, as it was her only *good* one ...

Laurie Has she only one good glove then?

Jo No, but you see she lent me the other one and then I managed to get coffee all over it. But I lent her one of mine which was stained with lemonade, and she didn't wear that.

Laurie begins to look confused

Oh, well, never mind, it's rather too involved to explain, but if a glove does turn up it belongs to Meg.

Laurie (*gallantly*) If it is to be found then I will recover it!

Jo Thank you, Laurie. I'm sorry to bother you, but as she is staying in bed today she has nothing to do but fret about things like that. How about another piece of cake? It's good, isn't it?

They rise and move to the table. Having helped themselves, Jo moves to the fire, leaving Laurie by the table

As she leaves the table, she fails to notice Mr Laurence descending the stairs, followed by Marmee. They reach the archway in time to hear Jo's words as she looks into the fire

Laurie, his mouth full of fruit cake, sees them first and stops eating, but is unable to warn her

You know, Laurie, it's a funny thing, but I thought I was going to be afraid of your grandfather. He looks very austere and forbidding, but he has kind eyes, though his mouth is grim, and he looks as if he had a tremendous will of his own. Mind you, I don't think he's as handsome as *my* grandfather, but I like him all the same. It seems to me that he. ... (*Her voice trails away as something in the air tells her that they are not alone. For a moment, she does not dare to turn and look, but, steeling herself, she turns slowly to face the tall figure now in the room, and regarding her severely*) Oh, well, I guess ... (*Her voice trails away once more*)

Mr Laurence So, you're not afraid of me after all, hey?

Jo (*choked with a mixture of fruit cake and confusion*) Not much, sir.

Mr Laurence But you don't think me as handsome as your grandfather, hey?

Jo Not quite, sir.

Mr Laurence And I've got a tremendous will of my own, have I?

Jo (*wincing*) I only said I thought so.

Mr Laurence And I look austere and forbidding, do I?
Jo Just a little, sir.
Mr Laurence But you like me, in spite of it all.
Jo (*a little spirit returning*) Yes, I do, sir.
Mr Laurence (*after a pause, then with a laugh*) Capital! You've got your grandfather's spirit, if you haven't his face! Well, Mrs March, here's one of your daughters who is not afraid of me—and even approves—with reservations.

The front door bell rings

Hannah appears to open it

And now, ma'am we must make our adieux. Come, Laurie, my boy, we must not overstay our welcome in this hospitable home. Goodbye, Mrs March, and again thank you for receiving me. I hope we shall be seeing more of each other.

Hannah re-appears followed by Brooke who is carrying a small posy of flowers which he hastily puts behind him when he sees the others

Hannah Mr John Brooke.

Hannah exits to the kitchen

Mr Laurence Ah, Brooke! Have you come to collect your pupil?
Brooke No, sir, I was passing and thought I would call to enquire after Miss March.
Mr Laurence 'Pon my soul, ma'am, I do declare that you and your young ladies have taken my entire household by storm! (*He spies the posy which Brooke has endeavoured to conceal*) What's this? And flowers too! Bless me, such gallantry!

Laughing good-naturedly Mr Laurence exits to the front door

Brooke (*blushing slightly*) Just a little nosegay to cheer the invalid, Mrs March, that is all.
Marmee How kind of you, Mr Brooke! I will just see Mr Laurence out and then I will be with you, please make yourself at home.

Marmee exits to Mr Laurence in the hall

Jo and Laurie move up to follow them

Laurie Goodbye for now, Jo; I'll have a thorough search for that glove and see if I can find it.

The party moves out of sight to the front door amid general "goodbyes" etc.

On Laurie's last remark Brooke, unseen by the others, has reacted. As they disappear he sets down the posy on the tea table, looks over his shoulder to make sure he is alone, and then draws from an inside pocket a lady's white evening glove. He looks at it with something akin to reverence and, as the Lights slowly fade, carefully restores it to its resting place

CURTAIN

ACT II

SCENE 1

The same. Several months later. Late afternoon

The warm glow of the summer sun now fills the parlour and the furniture has been rearranged to suit the season. There are vases of flowers to brighten the room

When the Lights come up Marmee is seated near the window in the sunshine, busy at her sewing

Beth, with Amy beside her to turn the pages of the music, is coming to the end of "Brahms' Cradle Song" which she is playing on a small cabinet piano that is new to the room since we last saw it

On a chair near the archway sits Hannah who has paused in her domestic routine to listen for a few moments to the musical interlude

Marmee (*as Beth finishes playing*) Thank you, Beth dear, you play more beautifully than ever.

Beth So much of that is due to Mr Laurence—letting me go over and practise on his grand piano all these months. That helped me improve such a lot, but, then, to give me this! (*She runs her hand affectionately along the key-board*) Although I've had it for a whole week now, I can hardly believe it!

Marmee He has been wonderfully kind. And to have given you the piano that once belonged to his own little daughter makes it a very special gift.

Hannah Wish I might die, if it ain't just about the handsomest present I ever did see! Not that the dear lamb don't deserve it!

Marmee I think Mr Laurence was very touched by those slippers you made for him, Beth.

Beth They were just something to thank him for all his kindness to me. I thought slippers might give him both comfort and pleasure.

Hannah And *such* slippers, too! My, how you worked at them! I declare it must have taken a tidy lot of patience just to embroider all them little, mauve pansy-flowers.

Amy (*ever the pedant*) They're not "pansy-flowers", Hannah! They're heart's-ease.

Hannah (*unaffected by the passing scorn*) So, they've gotten some other fancy name! That don't make 'em no easier to embroider, do it?

Amy (*choosing to ignore such mundane reasoning*) Oh, Beth, *do* read Mr Laurence's letter again! I just love to hear it.

Beth takes up an envelope which has been lying on the piano, and takes out a sheet of notepaper. It is obviously very precious to her

Beth (*reading*) "Miss March. Dear Madam . . .

Amy (*immediately interrupting with a cry of delight*) Oh! Doesn't that sound elegant! I wish someone would write to me like that!

Marmee (*gently reproving*) Amy, do you want to hear the letter or don't you?

Amy puts her hand over her mouth and nods her head

Go on, Beth, dear.

Beth "I have had many pairs of slippers in my life, but I have never had any that suited me so well as yours. Heart's-ease . . .

Amy casts a triumphant look at Hannah who is quite unrepentant

. . . is my favourite flower, and these will always remind me of the gentle giver. I like to pay my debts, so I know you will allow "the old gentleman" to send you something which once belonged to the little daughter he lost. With hearty thanks and best wishes, I remain your grateful friend and humble servant, James Laurence."

Beth carefully restores the letter to its envelope, and puts it back on the piano

Amy "Your humble servant!" Isn't that just so gracious and refined! Do you suppose I shall ever be addressed like that?

Hannah (*drily, as she prepares to return to her kitchen*) Well, I guess it don't cost none to *hope*. Land sakes—look at the time! I must get back to putting up them preserves or it'll never be done! Thank you for the music, Miss Beth, it was real pretty.

She exits to the kitchen

Marmee Mr Laurence has become a very dear friend to us in these last few months, and he takes as much interest in you girls as if you were his own. Naturally that pleases me, but I am glad also for his sake—it has brought him out of his seclusion a little.

Meg enters from the front door looking very pretty in a summer dress and bonnet

Come in, Meg dear.

Amy Hallo, Meg. Where have you been calling in your best dress and bonnet.

Meg (*removing her bonnet and moving to the window seat where she sits*) At Mrs Gardiner's. They have been telling me all about Belle Moffat's wedding. Apparently, it was a very splendid affair and the honeymoon is being spent in Paris. Just think how romantic that must be!

Beth Do you envy her, Meg?

Meg I'm afraid I do.

Amy (*bluntly*) Jo will be pleased.

Meg (*puzzled*) What do you mean?

Amy She says that if you care about riches you will never go and marry a poor man.

Meg (*flushing angrily*) I shall never "go and marry" anyone!

Amy Jo thinks so; she thinks that Mr Brooke is trying . . .

Marmee (*intervening diplomatically*) That will do, Amy. What Jo means is
that she is so fond of us as a united family, that she cannot bear to think
of our being parted—even by marriage. But, of course, that must come in
due time.

Beth Won't you mind it, Mother?

Marmee I shall mind it very much, Beth, but it is only the natural order of
things, my dear. Nothing would give me greater pleasure than to see you
all well and wisely married, leading useful pleasant lives with as little care
and sorrow to try you as God sees fit to send. To be loved and chosen by a
good man is the best and sweetest thing which can happen to a woman,
and I sincerely hope that my daughters may know that beautiful
experience. I am ambitious for you, of course, but not to have you make a
dash in the world—to marry rich men merely because they are rich. I'd
rather see you poor men's wives, if you were happy, beloved and
contented, than queens on thrones without self-respect or peace of mind.

Meg Belle says that poor girls don't stand any chance unless they put
themselves forward.

Amy Then we'll be old maids.

Marmee (*with a smile*) Well, Amy, better to be happy old maids than
unhappy wives or unmaidenly girls running out to get husbands. (*To
Meg*) Don't be troubled, Meg, poverty seldom daunts a sincere lover.
Leave these things to time my dear.

*A look of understanding passes between them, and then Marmee changes the
subject*

Where is Jo? She is late back from Aunt March today, isn't she?

Beth Yes, she said something about having to go into town on her way
home. She made it sound rather mysterious.

Amy She's been behaving very oddly the last week or two, I can't make it
out. She rushes to the door whenever the postman comes and then moons
about if there is no letter for her; and she and Laurie are forever
whispering together in corners as if they were up to something.

Meg I don't know when they are not up to something. Jo has always been a
harum-scarum, but since we've known Laurie she seems to have been a
thousand times worse. Only yesterday, I found them having a contest to
see who could leap the highest over the gate into the meadow!

Amy (*shocked*) Oh! How very unladylike!

Marmee (*amused*) I am sure that they are very good for each other. Jo, at
last, has the brother she has always wanted, and Laurie is far happier than
he used to be. (*More thoughtfully*) But I must admit that Jo has certainly
seemed rather restless lately.

Amy (*who hates to be left out of anything*) What do you think that means,
Marmee? I think we ought to . . .

Meg (*looking out of the window*) Here she comes! Oh, Mother, really—she's
running along like a wild thing with her bonnet hanging down her back
and all her ribbons flying—and there's Laurie chasing along after her!

Amy (*who has hurried to the window*) Why on earth is she waving that
newspaper in the air like a flag?

Meg What shall we do with that girl? She never will behave like a young lady.

Amy returns to her seat with a very superior air of resignation

Amy It's very trying. I wish she'd be a little more "commy la fo".

Marmee Now, my dear, you shouldn't want to alter your sister; we all have our own individual characters—*and* failings. Besides, I rather fancy that Jo will grow out of her tomboyishness in a year or two.

There is a crash as the front door opens

   Jo flies in with Laurie at her heels. She is very much out of breath, her bonnet thrown back and, in her hand, a newspaper which she brandishes triumphantly

   Jo!

Jo Oh, Marmee, Marmee! Look, just look! (*This short speech having exhausted her, she collapses into a chair, holding out the paper to her mother*)

Marmee Well, really, Jo, whatever . . .

Laurie, also out of breath, takes the paper from Jo, and gives it to Marmee in an attempt to explain

Laurie Please forgive the noise, Mrs March, but we are just so excited by this that we . . . (*He has to give up the struggle also and can only point inarticulately at the paper*)

Marmee By what? (*She looks uncomprehendingly at the paper*)

Meg Jo, what are you talking about?

Beth What is it, Jo?

Amy Oh for goodness sake! What *has* happened?

Jo (*taking a second wind and pointing at something in the paper*) This, oh—this!

Marmee looks at the item indicated, reads for a moment, and begins to smile. The suspense is too much for the others

Meg What is it, Mother?

Amy Marmee, please read it out, please!

Marmee (*reading*) *The Rival Painters*. A charming story of the romantic world of art by Miss Josephine March!

Meg (*incredulously*) You?

Jo Mmm! Your little sister!

Amy takes the paper from her mother and reads

Beth I knew it! I knew it! (*She runs to Jo and hugs her*) Oh, my Jo, I am so proud.

Amy And it covers nearly a whole page! However much did you get for it?

Jo I didn't think they'd really publish it, and I said nothing about it because I didn't want anyone else to be disappointed. (*She realizes that her mother has said nothing*) Oh, Marmee, please say something. You aren't vexed, are you?

Marmee (*holding Jo to her*) Vexed? Oh, my dear Jo, I am just so thrilled and proud I hardly know what to say.

Meg Tell us what happened! How did you manage to get them to print it? Tell us what happened!

Beth Yes, oh yes. What *will* Father say when he hears!

Amy How much *did* you get for it, Jo?

Jo Stop jabbering, girls, and I'll tell you everything. As you know I've been scribbling away at stories and things ever since I could write. Well, the last year or so I've been working even harder and I finished seven or eight stories which were about as good as I could make them. I thought to myself, "There, I've done my best! If this won't suit, I shall have to wait till I can do better." But I *did* want to know if they were good enough to publish—so, about ten days ago, I picked out the two I liked the best, and, screwing up all my courage, went off to the newspaper office.

Laurie I saw her going in, and she was behaving *very* suspiciously—so I waited until she came out.

Jo He didn't have to wait long! The editor man was very brief, said he would read them and let me have his answer this week. I was out in the street again before I knew where I was, and being plagued by this wretched boy to know what I had been up to. Oh, Marmee, I just had to tell him to keep him quiet or he might have spoilt it all!

Beth Go on, Jo. What did the newspaper man say when you went back?

Amy Oh, yes, do tell us!

Jo He said he liked them both, but that the paper didn't pay beginners. They only printed the stories and reviewed them; it was good practice he said and when the beginners improved anyone would pay. So I let him have the two, and today the first has been published! Laurie's read it and thinks it good, and I've got six more stories upstairs and perhaps I might actually *sell* them!

Laurie Hurrah for Miss Josephine March, the Celebrated Authoress!

Everyone cheers and joins in renewed congratulations

Beth Please may we take it out to show Hannah? She'll be so surprised at what she calls "that Jo's doin's".

Amy Marmee, do please read it to us.

Marmee It will have to be in the kitchen then, for Hannah won't leave her preserves again, and I don't suppose you will be able to wait until she has finished.

Beth and Amy exit to the kitchen with the paper and cries of "Hannah!" "Look at this!" "What do you think Jo's done?" etc.

Marmee (*turning to Jo*) Jo, my dear, I am more proud of this than I can say. You have worked hard at your writing, and you deserve success. But, dear, don't let that success spoil you or the quality of your work.

Jo (*with all her heart*) Oh, I won't, Marmee, I won't. I only want to do the best I can always.

Marmee And I know that you will always try. (*She looks at the time*) Good gracious, it's getting late! You'll have to be leaving for the theatre soon, won't you? Jo, aren't you going to change and tidy yourself? Meg is dressed ready to go.

Jo Need I bother, Marmee? I loathe getting all dressed up to go anywhere, and I should be much more comfortable in these clothes.

Marmee Well, dear, that would not be much of a compliment to your escorts. At least run upstairs and put on your new bonnet—and you may borrow my little cream shawl to put over your shoulders, it is on the chair in my room.

Laurie That is about all you will have time for now.

Jo exits

The excitement over Jo's story has made me forgetful; I must go and see about the carriage at once or we shall be late.

Marmee (*moving with him to the door*) It is good of you and Mr Brooke to escort Meg and Jo. I know that they will enjoy it all the more in your company.

Laurie (*with a mock bow*) It is a privilege to be entrusted with such precious charges, ma'am!

Jo (*off, upstairs*) Christopher Columbus! Get along with you!

Laurie exits

Marmee turns back into the room

Marmee Now, I must go to the kitchen for this great reading ceremony. I am all curiosity to know more about *The Rival Painters* and their "Romantic World of Art"!

Jo precipitates herself down the stairs and into the room carrying the shawl and new bonnet

(*With a shake of the head*) That didn't take you long, Jo! I'll say goodbye now my dears, have a good time.

Marmee exits

The girls busy themselves getting ready for the forthcoming excursion. Meg, with a critical eye, adjusts her sister's bonnet and hair

Jo (*as she submits to these attentions*) I suppose Mr Brooke will be all courtesy and attention to you as usual.

Meg I am sure he is equally courteous and attentive to all of us—though he gets little enough encouragement from you, Jo. You are really very rude to him at times.

Jo I don't intend to encourage him. I think it was a great mistake of Marmee's allowing him to give you those German lessons. He seems always to be in and out of the house these days.

Meg So is Laurie for that matter.

Jo That's different. Laurie comes to see all of us, or to arrange for us to go on a picnic, or skating, or to the theatre where we can be all friends together. But Mr Brooke comes here just to look cow-eyed at you.

Meg Jo, you are most unjust! Why are you so much against him?

Jo Since you ask, I'll tell you. I've been watching him, and I believe he would like to take you away from us.

Meg What nonsense! How you do dramatize everything! (*A slight pause while Meg attempts to affect an air of indifference*) Not that there is anything in what you say, but supposing that the boot was on the other foot. You'd feel very differently if somebody came to take you away.

Jo (*vehemently*) I'd like to see them try it! (*Feeling that, perhaps, she has said too much*) I'm sorry, Meg, I am a silly, jealous thing, I suppose; but, you see, I love a few persons very dearly and I dread to lose their affection or have it lessened in any way.

The sisters squeeze each other's hands in affectionate understanding, and then Jo briskly changes the subject

I *am* looking forward to this visit to the theatre. Do you realize it will be the first time that we have been without the others? It's quite an adventure!

Meg (*her face clouding*) Yes, but I am afraid I feel a little guilty.

Jo Why, for goodness sake?

Meg You see, I haven't had the heart to tell Amy that we are going without her.

Jo Why ever not?

Meg She is a little jealous of some of the privileges we enjoy as older girls, and I thought she would fret if she knew she hadn't been invited.

Jo She'll have to know sooner or later, and, anyway, she's going to the theatre with Beth and Hannah next week. Besides, she's had a cold and I know Marmee doesn't want her to go out just yet.

Meg I know, but ...

Amy enters from the kitchen

Amy (*as she enters*) Come on, Meg, aren't you coming to hear the story? Marmee's just going to read it to us and we are ... (*noticing that Meg and Jo are dressed for outdoors*) Where are you two going?

Jo (*anxious to avoid a scene*) Never mind, little girls shouldn't ask questions.

Amy (*bridling slightly*) Do tell me! I think you might let me know!

Meg (*cautiously*) Well, dear, you see, Jo and I have been invited ...

Jo Now, Meg, be quiet or you will spoil it all. You can't go, Amy, so don't be a baby and whine about it.

Amy You're going somewhere with Laurie, I know you are. You were whispering and laughing together last night when I came in here, and you stopped when you saw me. You *are* going somewhere with him, aren't you?

Jo Yes we are; now do be still and stop bothering.

Meg We are going with Mr Brooke and Laurie to the theatre.

Amy Let me go, too! I've got some money and Mother said I might go. It was mean not to tell me in time. Oh, please let me go!

Jo There you are! I knew she'd make a scene.

Meg Just listen to me a minute and be a good child. Mother doesn't wish you to go out this week as you have had a bad cold and it's not quite well yet. Next week you can go with Beth and Hannah, as arranged.

Amy I don't like that half as well as going with you and Laurie and Mr Brooke in the carriage. Please let me! I've been shut up with this cold for ever so long, and I'm dying for some fun. Beth's had her piano given to her, and Jo's had all the excitement about the story, and now you're off to the theatre, and I haven't had anything. It just isn't fair! Do take me, Meg! I'll be ever so good.

Meg (*touched by the appeal*) Suppose we take her, Jo? I don't believe Mother would mind if we wrapped her up well.

Jo (*with finality*) If she goes I shan't; and if I don't, Laurie won't like it. Besides it would be very rude to go and drag in Amy when only we have been invited. I should think she'd hate to poke herself in where she isn't wanted.

Amy I shall go! Meg says I may, and if I pay for myself then no one else has anything to do with it.

Jo You can't sit with us for our seats are reserved, and you mustn't sit alone. Laurie or Mr Brooke would have to give you their place, and that would spoil our pleasure; or they'd get another seat for you, and that wouldn't be proper, when you weren't asked. You shan't stir a step; so you may just stay where you are.

Amy starts to cry. Jo is obviously adamant. Meg, still hoping to pacify all concerned, turns to Amy

Meg Now, Amy dear, do try to understand. You see Mr Brooke and Laurie did ask us to go with them, and, anyway, you'll . . .

Jo (*at the window*) Here's the carriage! Come on, Meg, we're late already. Leave the silly girl to her tantrum.

They move to the archway

Amy (*looking up, a threatening note in her voice*) You'll be sorry for this, Jo March! You see if you're not!

Jo (*hustling Meg out*) Oh, fiddlesticks!

Meg and Jo exit

Left alone, Amy sobs angrily then moves to the sofa, punching the cushions in her childish rage. Suddenly she stops, thinks quickly for a moment, then, with a malicious glint in her eyes, she rises and moves, full of purpose, towards the stairs as . . .

The Lights slowly fade to Black-out

SCENE 2

The same. The following day. Early evening

When the Lights come up Beth and Amy are playing cards. A game has just finished, and Beth is gathering the cards from the table

Amy, still holding a few cards, rises, dropping them on the table, and moves to the fireplace. She is preoccupied and ill-at-ease. Beth is aware that something is wrong

Amy (*as she moves*) I don't want to play any more just now.

Pause

Beth (*after stealing several glances at Amy*) Is anything the matter, Amy? You have been so quiet and withdrawn all day.

Amy (*without looking at her sister*) No, I'm all right. I expect it's this cold—I still have it about me a bit.

Beth I wondered if you were very upset after that dreadful quarrel you had with Jo yesterday. We could hear you shouting when we were out in the kitchen.

Amy (*defensively*) Well, she vexed me beyond endurance.

Beth It was difficult for Meg and Jo, you know, when Mr Brooke and Laurie had asked only them to go.

Amy Yes, I know; but Jo needn't have been so horrid about it.

Meg enters with a bowl of roses

Meg Aren't these lovely? Poor Father, it is a shame, just when his rose bushes are more beautiful than they have ever been, he's far away and can't see them (*She sets the bowl down on the piano*) Has the postman been?

Beth Not yet, I think the mail must be late.

Meg It must be; it's our day for a letter from Father, and his letters are as regular as the sun. Where is everyone?

Beth Marmee is turning out the linen cupboard, and Jo has just gone up to her attic. Wasn't that a splendid story of hers, *The Rival Painters*? I am so pleased that she's had something published at last. It will . . .

Jo suddenly appears, bouncing downstairs, an anxious expression on her face

Jo Has anyone taken my book?

Meg What book, Jo?

Jo Why, the manuscript of my six other stories. I copied them all out ready in case they should be wanted and made them up into a little book. I left it on my desk, but it's gone; I've searched everywhere but I just can't find it. Are you sure you haven't seen it anywhere?

Meg No, I'm afraid not.

Beth Oh, Jo, how dreadful! Are you quite sure you left it up there?

Jo Quite. (*She notices Amy's silence*) Amy, you've got it.

Amy (*still facing the fireplace*) No, I haven't.

Jo You know where it is then.

Amy No, I don't.

Jo (*moving to her*) That's a fib.

Amy (*turning to face Jo*) It isn't. I haven't got it and I don't know where it is now, and I don't care.

Jo (*taking her by the arms*) You know something about it, and you'd better tell at once or I'll make you.

Amy Scold as much as you like, you'll never see your silly old book again.

Jo (*alarmed*) Why not? What do you mean?

Amy (*looking her sister in the face*) Because I've burnt it.

There is a pause while the full meaning of this statement strikes home. Jo's hands fall away from Amy's arms

Jo (*hardly believing her*) What! My stories that I've worked at so hard. You've burnt them—now, just when I might be able to sell them.

Amy Yes! I have! I told you I'd make you pay for being so cross and horrid yesterday, and I have, so . . .

Jo (*grasping Amy and shaking her*) You wicked, wicked girl! I shall never be able to write them again!

Amy Let me go you beast! You only had what you deserved!

Amy and Jo struggle, their voices rise. Meg and Beth move forward to part them as . . .

Marmee appears on the stairs and enters the room

A moment later Hannah, also alarmed by the noise, appears in the archway

Marmee (*as she enters*) Jo! Amy! Stop it at once! Whatever is going on? You ought to be ashamed of yourselves! Jo, I am surprised at such behaviour!

Jo (*almost in tears*) She's burnt the manuscript of my six other stories. It was the only copy I had, and she's burnt it!

Tears finally overtaking her, she exits hurriedly upstairs

Marmee Amy! What have you done! Those stories were the pride of Jo's heart; she has worked at them patiently, putting her whole heart into her work, hoping to produce something good enough to print. You have destroyed the loving work of several years. Why, Amy? Why? Was it something to do with that quarrel you had yesterday?

Amy (*full of remorse*) Oh, yes, Marmee. I did it in a fit of anger, and I've felt dreadful ever since. Whatever am I to do?

Marmee First, you must beg Jo's pardon, and then we must see what can be done to make some sort of amends. Beth, dear, would you go and fetch Jo, please?

Before Beth can move, Jo reappears on the stairs. She has thrown on a bonnet and shawl, and is busy putting on her gloves

Marmee (*seeing her*) Where are you going, Jo?

Jo Out, Marmee, I must go out and walk or I shall burst.

Marmee (*looking at Amy*) Before you go, dear, I think Amy has something to say to you.

Amy (*very humbly*) Please forgive me, Jo: I'm very, very sorry. I promise I . . .

Jo I shall never forgive you as long as I live.

Marmee Jo, my dear, don't go out in anger like this. I appeal to you to forgive your sister and make things right between you.

Jo It was an abominable thing to do, and she doesn't deserve to be forgiven.

Jo exits quickly

Amy, remorse and guilt again breaking over her, dissolves into tears

Marmee Now, Amy dear, you have done wrong and Jo is quite naturally full of anger; but, perhaps, after her walk she will feel better and then you must ask her again to forgive you and offer to ... (*she stops as ...*)

Jo re-appears from the front door, followed by Laurie who waits in the hall. All trace of anger has left her face, now there is only a look of anxiety and concern. In her hand she holds a telegram. Slowly she approaches her mother

Jo I met Laurie outside, Marmee. He's just come from the telegraph office, they gave him ... oh, Marmee. It's a telegram from Washington.

There is a pause while Marmee hesitates before taking the telegram. Then, pulling herself together, she opens and reads it

Everyone's attention is riveted on Marmee. Swaying slightly, she passes the telegram to Jo, and, with her hand to her temple, sits abruptly in her chair. Hannah, Meg and Beth move to her as Jo reads the telegram aloud

Jo "Your husband very ill with fever. Come at once. Medical Officer in Charge, Military Hospital, Washington."

For a moment there is silence. Amy and Beth are in tears. Suddenly Hannah, the first to recover, turns and smoothes down her apron

Hannah The Lord keep the dear man! (*Wiping her eyes briskly with the back of her hand*) I won't waste no time a'cryin' but start to get your things ready right away, mum.

She exits upstairs

Marmee (*rising*) Hannah is right; there is no time for tears now. Let us be calm, girls, and think what must be done. Where is Laurie?

Laurie (*coming forward from the hall*) Here, ma'am; oh, please let me do something to help!

Marmee Then, would you send a telegram to this address—(*she gives him the telegram*) saying that I will come at once. The next train leaves in about three hours' time. I shall take that.

Laurie Is there nothing else I can do? My horse is ready—I'll go anywhere, do anything.

Marmee Perhaps you would take a note to Aunt March? Jo, dear, give me a pen and paper.

Jo fetches paper and a pen from the cupboard. Marmee sits at the table and writes as she speaks

Meg, would you go and help Hannah bring down the black trunk from the attic, please? She won't be able to manage it alone, and then, perhaps, you and Beth would start to get out my clothes to pack?

Meg and Beth exit upstairs

Amy, dear, in the dining-room cupboard are those two bottles of old wine which Mr Laurence gave us at Christmas. I shall take them with me for father; he must have the best of everything.

Amy exits across the hall to the dining-room

Marmee completes her brief note, and seals it in an envelope

Jo (*as Marmee does this*) What am I to do to help, Marmee?

Marmee (*as she hastily addresses the envelope*) I want you to go down to the Soldiers' Aid Society and tell Mrs King what has happened. Explain to her that I have to go to Washington, and that I shall not be able to help for a while. And on the way I'd like you to get some things I shall need. (*She hands the letter to Laurie*) There, Laurie; now don't kill yourself riding at too desperate a pace, there is no need of that.

Laurie exits speedily

Marmee takes a fresh piece of paper to make a short list for Jo

I must go prepared for nursing, and these are things that may be required. Alas, hospital stores are not always good, and I don't want to be short of anything. (*She continues her list*)

Jo Marmee, you've written to ask Aunt March to lend you money, haven't you?

Marmee Yes, dear, I have not enough for so long a journey and I do not know how long I may have to be away. It is only as a loan and I'm not too proud to beg for your father.

Jo Oh, Marmee, if only I earned enough to be able to give you something to help, so that we didn't have to ask favours from Aunt March. She didn't approve of Father going to the war in the first place and now she'll be able to croak and say "I told you so!"

Amy returns with the wine during the next speech. She sets it down on the table and stands quietly listening

Marmee rises and moves to give Jo the list. She puts an arm around her and kisses her

Marmee Hush, dear, we should be grateful that we have her to turn to in time of distress. You shall help in paying it back later on; will that satisfy you? But away now on your errands, for time is precious and there is much to be done.

As Jo turns to go she sees Amy. Their eyes meet for a moment, Amy's eloquent in their appeal; suddenly Jo moves to Amy and takes her in her arms in silent forgiveness. Then Jo turns and moves up to the archway, pauses and looks back at her mother, who nods and smiles approvingly

Jo smiles back briefly and hurries out

Marmee moves to comfort Amy who has broken down once again under a mixture of remorse and relief, anxiety and joy

Jo (*off*) Good evening, Mr Laurence. Please go right in. Mother is in the parlour, she will be glad to see you.

Mr Laurence enters

Marmee kisses Amy and gently sends her upstairs

Amy exits

Mr Laurence (*as he enters*) My dear lady, Laurie has told me your news. I am so very distressed, and have come over to know if there is anything I can do to be of service? I have taken the liberty of arranging for the carriage to take you and your boxes to the station when you are ready, but is there any other way in which I may help?

Marmee Thank you, Mr Laurence, but I think not.

Mr Laurence May I, perhaps, offer myself as escort? The journey to Washington for a lady travelling alone ...

Marmee My dear friend, thank you from my heart, but I will not hear of it. True, anxiety ill fits one for travelling, but it is a long way and I fear that you would find it too exhausting.

Mr Laurence Well, well, we will see what can be done, for I am not easy in my mind that you should travel alone.

Marmee Please do not worry. You will give me greater ease of heart by remaining here and keeping a watchful eye on my little family while I am away from them.

Mr Laurence That I will do and gladly. I will look after them as if they were my own.

Marmee (*laying a hand gratefully on his arm*) You are our good friend.

Mr Laurence (*putting his hand over hers*) Be comforted, dear lady. There is always light behind the clouds.

Marmee (*her control faltering in the face of his sympathy*) Oh, Mr Laurence! I feel I must open my heart to someone! I have not dared to admit it to the girls, for I do not wish to distress them any more than is necessary ... but, though I have hope, I pray that I may not be ... too late.

Mr Laurence comforts her as ...

The Lights fade for a moment

When the Lights come up some two hours have passed and the initial shock has softened a little. Everyone is still busy with the preparations for Marmee's departure; Hannah and Laurie are descending the stairs with Marmee's trunk

Hannah (*as the trunk is set down in the hall*) Thank you, Mr Laurie. Now I must finish a'packin' that basket of vittles for Mrs March's journey. She'll need a bite to eat, goin' all that way.

Laurie Is Jo back yet, Hannah?

Hannah No, she ain't. Blessed if I know where that harum-scarum's got to. I want to close up that box of medicines, but I can't do it till she comes with them things her Ma sent her out to get.

Laurie But that was nearly two hours ago! Where *can* she be? I think I'll go down the road and see if she's coming.

The front door bell rings

Oh, perhaps that's her now!

Hannah Don't reckon as how she'd ring the bell. Would you see who it is, Mr Laurie, please?

Laurie exits to the front door

Hannah turns to exit to the kitchen, talking as she goes

There's a tidy lot to do yet, and Mrs March will have to think about getting ready to go soon.

Hannah exits to the kitchen as we hear Laurie's voice at the front door

Laurie (*off*) Oh, hallo, Mr Brooke! Would you go in—someone will be down in a minute for sure, I'm just off to look for Jo.

Brooke enters; he is carrying a portmanteau, overcoat and hat, and is obviously prepared for a journey. He looks around the parlour but finding no one there, turns back into the hall to put down his belongings. As he turns back from doing so, he almost collides with Meg who enters from the kitchen carrying a small tray of tea things

Meg (*almost dropping the tray*) Oh, Mr Brooke!

Brooke catches the corners of the tray nearest to him to prevent its falling

Brooke Miss March, I'm extremely sorry to hear the news of your father. I have come to offer myself as escort to your mother. Mr Laurence has some commissions for me in Washington, and it would give me real satisfaction to be of service to Mrs March while I am there.

They stand very close, only the tray dividing them

Meg How kind you all are! Mother will accept I am sure, and it will be such a relief to know that she has someone to take care of her. Thank you very much!

For a moment, they stand looking into each other's eyes, without speaking, until Meg's self-consciousness re-asserts itself. She disengages the tray from Brooke's hands, and moves into the room. Meg is embarrassed; Brooke unsure of how far he should declare himself. They take refuge in social pleasantry

Won't you sit down, Mr Brooke? I've just made Mother some tea, perhaps you would like to join her? A hot drink will help to fortify you for your journey.

Beth and Amy enter from the kitchen carrying between them Hannah's "basket of vittles"; this they set down by the other luggage in the hall

Brooke (*as he takes a seat*) Thank you, I should like that.

Amy (*entering the parlour*) There's Mother's "basket of vittles" as Hannah calls it. I should think there is enough food there to feed a family for a fortnight. (*She suddenly sees Brooke, smiles and bobs a little curtsy to him*) Good evening, Mr Brooke.

As Beth enters behind her, Amy looks from Meg to Brooke and back again. A little smirk appears on her face

Beth (*not immediately noticing Brooke*) It's not only for the journey, Amy. Hannah has packed all sorts of good things for Father to make him well again. (*Seeing Brooke and curtseying*) Oh! Good-evening, Mr Brooke.

Brooke (*pleasantly*) Good-evening, Beth. Good-evening, Amy.

There is a slightly awkward pause. No one says anything, but Amy and Beth exchange looks and smother a giggle

Meg (*rather too brightly*) Mr Brooke has come to escort Mother to Washington. Isn't that splendid?

A further pause, a further look, a further suppressed giggle. In desperation Meg decides positive action is needed. Her voice hardens a little

Meg Amy, dear, would you go upstairs, please, and tell Mother that Mr Brooke is here, and that I have made some tea for her?

Amy exits upstairs struggling to suppress yet another giggle

Beth, left on her own, reverts to her normal shyness, uncertain what to do. Meg has a sudden inspiration

Oh, Beth, Mr Brooke would like some tea also, would you fetch another cup and saucer, please?

Thankful for an excuse to go, Beth bobs another little curtsey and exits to the kitchen

To cover her confusion, Meg busies herself re-arranging the teatray as she speaks

We are going to miss you both very much, Mr Brooke. It will seem very strange here without Mother, and without your calling to see us. (*Accidently, she knocks a teaspoon onto the floor, and stoops to retrieve it*)

Brooke immediately follows suit. They grasp the spoon together, and, for a moment or two, remain half-kneeling

Brooke (*as they kneel*) I, too, am going to miss coming to see you . . . er . . . all of you . . . very much.

Their eyes meet. For a moment longer the picture is held. They seem about to speak when there is the sound of the front door opening

Laurie enters

They rise quietly and without confusion

Laurie speaks as he enters. He is too concerned about Jo to be aware of anything betweeen Meg and Brooke at that moment

Laurie There's no sign of Jo anywhere! I can't think why she's so late for she didn't have far to go. I don't want to alarm your mother, Meg, but I am beginning to wonder ...

His words are cut short by the appearance of Marmee carrying her cloak and bonnet, who descends the stairs with Amy

Beth re-appears with the cup and saucer

Marmee Amy has been telling me the reason for your call, Mr Brooke; how very kind of you to offer to act as my escort. I may say it is a great comfort and relief, for I was not looking forward to so long a journey alone.

Meg pours the tea

Meg Your tea, Marmee (*she hands her a cup and offers one to Mr Brooke*), and Mr Brooke.

Brooke Thank you. I am most happy to be of service, Mrs March, but had it not been for some business in Washington which Mr Laurence is anxious for me to attend to on his behalf, it would have ...

Marmee (*seeing through this gentle subterfuge*) Ah, I see, then we must be grateful to Mr Laurence for so conveniently remembering those commissions just at this time, I have true friends, indeed!

Hannah enters from the kitchen

Hannah Excuse me, mum, I've more or less finished a'packin' everythin', and as soon as I gits them medicines and things from Miss Jo I can close the hospital box.

Laurie moves to look out of the window

Marmee Isn't Jo back? But she should have been here long before this! Oh, Meg, you don't think that ...

Meg No, Marmee, of course not, she'll turn up all right.

Laurie I think she's coming now—yes—it is her! It's all right, Mrs March, she's safe and sound—and in a careering hurry, as usual!

Laurie hurries out to let Jo in

There are general exclamations of relief

Jo appears in the archway, very much out of breath and "with a very queer expression of countenance—a mixture of fun and fear, satisfaction and regret". For a moment she looks around the room struggling to get her breath as she passes the parcel of medical supplies to Hannah

Marmee Jo, dear, I was beginning to get worried, you have been such a long time and ...

Her words are cut short as Jo moves to her, and, pulling her hand from her pocket, puts a roll of dollar bills on the table beside her mother

Jo That's my contribution, Marmee, towards making Father better and bringing him home safe and sound.

There is a brief silence while everyone stares unbelievingly at the money

Marmee (*taking it in her hands*) Twenty-five dollars! My dear, where did you get it?

Jo (*still a little strange as she loosens the ribbons on her bonnet*) It's mine; I came by it honestly; I didn't beg, borrow or steal it, I earned it—and I don't think you'll blame me, for I only sold what was my own. (*She pulls off her bonnet and turns suddenly. Her long, abundant hair has been cut short*)

Meg Your hair! Your beautiful hair! You've had it cut off.

Amy Oh, Jo, how could you? It was your one beauty!

Beth (*running to her*) She doesn't look like my Jo any more, but I love her dearly for it!

Laurie Well done, Jo! It makes you more boyish than ever!

Marmee (*holding out her hand*) My dear Jo, there was no need of this!

Jo takes her mother's hand, relieved that the confession is over, and assumes an air of indifference as she rumples her cropped head

Jo It doesn't affect the fate of the nation, so don't wail about it, please! It will be good for my vanity—I was getting far too proud of my hair—and it will freshen up my brains to have that mop taken off. So please take the money, Marmee, and say no more about it.

Marmee I can't be cross, for I think I can guess what it cost you to make such a sacrifice, but I should like to know a little more about it.

Amy Whatever made you do it? I don't think I could bear to part with any of my hair.

Jo Well, I was wild to do something for Father. I thought how nice it would be if Marmee could have something extra which she didn't expect. I was determined to make some money if I sold the nose off my face to get it!

Marmee But, my dear, I'm afraid that you will regret it one of these days.

Jo No, Marmee, I won't. (*Rather enjoying it as she settles down to tell her story*) I hadn't the least idea of selling my hair at first, but then, in a barber's window, I saw tails of hair with the prices marked. It came to me all of a sudden that I had one thing to make money out of, and, without stopping to think, I walked in, asked if they bought hair, and what they would give for mine.

Beth I don't know how you dared to do it.

Laurie What did the barber have to say?

Jo He rather stared at first as if he wasn't used to having girls bounce into his shop and ask him to buy their hair. Then he said he didn't care about mine, it wasn't the fashionable colour, he never paid much for it in the first place, the work put into it made it dear, and so on, and so on. Well, it was getting late, so I begged him to take it, and told him why I was in such a hurry. It was a silly thing to do, I dare say, but it changed his mind and he agreed to take it for twenty-five dollars.

Meg Didn't you feel dreadful when he started to cut it off?

Jo (*with a bravado that she doesn't quite feel*) Oh! I never snivel over trifles like that! (*Rather more soberly*) I will confess, though, that I felt odd when

I saw the dear old hair laid out on the table, and felt only the short ends on my head. The man saw me looking at it, and picked out a long lock for me to keep. (*Producing it from her pocket with a flourish*) I'll give it to you, Marmee, as a little reminder of past glories—for a crop is so comfortable that I don't think I shall ever have a mane again!

Marmee (*quietly*) Thank you, my dear. (*She takes the lock of hair tenderly and puts it into her reticule*)

The others, apart from Brooke, cluster around Jo, talking together

Meg Jo, I think you have been very brave!

Amy Oh, yes, it must have been nearly as bad as having a tooth out.

Beth It was a lovely thought—to give something of your own to help Father.

Hannah Won't take such a tidy time to wash and dry your hair now!

Laurie Good old Jo. I think it was a wonderful idea!

Brooke (*crossing to Marmee*) Forgive me for intruding, ma'am, but the train leaves in less than an hour. I think that, perhaps, Laurie and I should get your boxes out on to the porch ready to load on to the carriage—it will be here shortly.

Marmee Oh, yes, of course; thank you so much, Mr Brooke. I can tell that you are going to be a great help to me.

Brooke, taking Laurie with him, goes out to the hall and starts to remove the trunks, etc.

Hannah (*suddenly remembering the parcel in her arms*) Lawdy! The hospital box!

She exits to the kitchen in great haste

Marmee (*taking up her cloak and bonnet*) My dears, I must soon be starting my journey. I leave you in Hannah's care and Mr Laurence's protection. Hannah is faithfulness itself and our good neighbour will guard you as if you were his own. I have no fears for you, yet I am anxious that you should take this trouble in the right spirit. Don't grieve and fret while I am away; go on with your work as usual, for work is a solace and help at these times. Hope, and keep busy; in any perplexity go to Mr Laurence; write to me often, and do all you can to help and cheer each other.

The sad reality of the moment strikes the girls in different ways, but their replies come all together, overlapping each other

Meg   ⎫   ⎧ Yes, Mother, of course we will.
Jo   ⎬ (*together*) ⎨ We will, Marmee, we will!
Beth   We shall miss you so much, Marmee.
Amy   ⎭   ⎩ We'll be good, Marmee. Promise!

Marmee (*striving to be cheerful for their sakes*) Now, my dears, before I go, shall we sing one of our evening hymns together as usual, eh? Which shall it be?

Beth crosses to the piano

Meg Oh, let it be Father's favourite!

They gather quietly around the piano. Beth begins to play, and the others to join in the hymn as their arms encircle the mother who is leaving them. Bravely, five voices are raised in song. However, as the first verse comes to an end, Jo stops singing and breaks away from the group. As the second verse starts, she suddenly breaks down completely and weeps. The others stop, and Marmee moves to her

Marmee Jo, my dear, what is it? Are you crying because of Father?

Jo (*sobbing*) No, Marmee, not now.

Marmee What then, my dear?

Jo (*raising her head and with a great sob*) Well ... it's my ... it's ... it's my hair!

Marmee nods to the others to resume the hymn, in which she joins, as she continues to comfort the unhappy Jo

As the singing continues, the Lights fade gently

CURTAIN

ACT III

The same. A Sunday in November. Morning

The room has been re-arranged to its winter setting

When the Lights come up Meg, in an apron, is busily dusting. Jo is deeply absorbed in a letter she is writing. For a few moments they pursue their tasks industriously, then Meg, straightening herself, glances out of the window at the grey light

Meg I think November is the most disagreeable month in the whole year!

Jo (*pausing in her writing*) And without Marmee here it seems a hundred times worse. She's been away nearly three months now, but it still feels as though half the house is missing.

Meg I am beginning to get used to it, but, at first, I felt as though there had been an earthquake. Well, I suppose I'd better get on! (*She briskly resumes her work*)

Jo Whatever are you fussing about with a duster for on a Sunday morning? I cleaned this room thoroughly only yesterday.

Meg Yes, Jo, I know you did, but you forget that Aunt March said she would call on her way home from morning service—"to see how we are getting on". I am just *not* going to give her the chance to say that we aren't looking after things properly, and if there's a speck of dust anywhere she'll spot it.

Jo Oh, fiddlesticks to Aunt March! I can't see that it matters to her if we are all knee-deep in dust.

Meg It matters to me! How are you getting on with the weekly dispatch to Washington?

Jo I have only a few more lines to write and then you can add your instalment. (*As she resumes her writing*) I've told Marmee how thrilled we are that Father is at last gaining strength. I must say that, though it made me absolutely bilious to see the way Mr Brooke used to moon around you before he went away, he was a real trump to telegraph to us the minute Father took a turn for the better.

The mention of Brooke causes Meg to pause once more in her work

Meg He is so thoughtful, and what a help he has been to Mother and Father! You know, Jo, when I saw him standing by Marmee, just before they left, he looked so strong and sensible and kind that he made me think of Mr Greatheart in *Pilgrim's Progress*.

Jo Oh, Christmas! I should have known better than to bring his name up. There I've finished! Shall I get on with the dusting while you write your messages?

They exchange occupations

Amy, also in an apron, appears from the kitchen

Amy Where's Beth? She said she was coming to help Hannah and me do the vegetables for dinner.

Jo (*dusting with more vigour than finesse*) She went to call on the Hummels after we'd been to early service this morning. I don't suppose she's back yet.

Amy I think she is, for I heard her come in some time ago, but I don't know what's happened to her since then.

Jo Oh, I expect she's busy upstairs.

Amy exits to the hall, calls "Beth" once or twice, receives no reply, and exits to the kitchen

Meg (*looking up from writing, an anxious note in her voice*) I hope Beth is all right. She's not been looking very well these last few days. I am afraid that she's been doing too much since Mother went away, but she's always so anxious to help and do what she calls "her fair share".

Jo Yes, but the trouble is she does a great deal more than her fair share, and a good many other things as well. The Hummels, for instance; she visits them regularly.

Meg (*guiltily*) Yes, the Hummels. You know, Jo, we promised Mother that we wouldn't forget them, and that we would visit them, especially when the cold weather came. I believe Beth is the only one of us who has kept that promise.

Jo (*defensively*) Well, there's always so much to do at home here, besides our ordinary work.

Meg Mother always found time to spare for them, and Beth has been just as busy as the rest of us. She did ask me to go with her last week. She said something about the baby not being well and not being sure what to do for it, but I was trying to finish off that new dress and said I couldn't manage to go just then.

Jo (*thoughtfully*) Yes, she told me the baby was poorly. I believe the eldest child, Lottchen, looks after it while Mrs Hummel goes out to work.

Meg (*with awakened concern*) But she is only twelve—and has all the other children to care for as well.

Beth appears on the stairs in the next speech. She descends slowly and a little uncertainly. Clearly something is wrong

Jo (*with sudden decision*) We'll go tomorrow and see what we can do to help. I wonder if we should ... Christopher Columbus! What's the matter, Beth? (*She moves to help her sister*)

Beth (*putting out a hand to ward her off*) You've both had scarlet fever, haven't you?

Meg Yes, years ago. Why, Beth? Aren't you well, dear?

Beth It's the baby—Mrs Hummel's poor little baby—it's ... it's d̲e̲a̲d̲.

Jo Dead!

Beth It died in my lap about an hour ago while I was nursing it.

Jo (*taking Beth in her arms*) Oh, my poor dear, how dreadful for you. Meg, why didn't one of us go?

Beth As soon as I got there I saw in a minute that the poor little mite was worse. Lottchen said that her mother had gone for the doctor. Two of the other children were sick as well, so I offered to nurse the baby while she attended to them; but all of a sudden it gave a little cry and trembled and then it lay very still. I tried to warm its feet, and Lottchen gave it some milk, but it didn't stir—and then I knew it must be dead. (*She cries softly, almost to herself*)

Meg (*comforting her*) Don't cry, dear, what did you do?

Beth I just sat and held the little body till Mrs Hummel came with the doctor. He examined it and said that the cause of death was scarlet fever, and that he should have been called before. Mrs Hummel told him that she was poor and had tried to cure the baby herself; then, suddenly, he told me to go home at once. He thinks I may have caught it too.

Jo Oh, Beth, if you should be sick I never could forgive myself! Meg, what shall we do?

Meg If only Mother were at home! You've been in to see the baby several times this last week, haven't you, Beth? And among the other children who are probably going to have the fever too. I'm afraid it's quite likely that you'll go down with it as well, dear. I'm going to call Hannah, she nursed Jo and me through it, and she'll know what to do. (*She turns to go*)

Beth (*as Meg turns*) Don't let Amy come in here, she's never had it and I should hate to pass it on to her.

Meg exits

(*Turning to Jo*) Are you quite sure that you and Meg can't have it over again?

Jo I don't think so—and, anyway, I don't care if I do. Serve me right, selfish pig, to let you go down to the Hummels alone when all I was doing was writing rubbish upstairs.

Beth You mustn't say that, Jo. It's not rubbish, your stories are being published now and ... (*She stops short and puts her hand to her head*) I think I'll go upstairs and lie down for a while.

Jo (*helping Beth to rise*) Are you feeling worse, pet?

Beth I feel rather hot and my head aches so—I shall be better lying down.

Hannah enters and moves straight to Beth

Hannah Land sakes, child, why didn't you tell me afore that you was a'feelin' ill?

Jo She's going up to bed, Hannah.

Hannah (*taking charge of Beth*) Best thing to do! I've told Miss Meg that, if it is the fever, I think we'd best pack Amy off to your Aunt March for a spell, to keep her out of harm's way. Now come along, my lamb; up to bed with you.

Hannah and Beth move towards the stairs

The front door bell rings

Jo All right, Hannah. I'll see who it is.

Jo goes to the front door

Laurie's voice is heard in greeting

Hannah and Beth exit upstairs

Jo hustles Laurie into the parlour

Laurie (*as he is pushed in*) Steady on, Jo! What's going on?

Jo You've had scarlet fever, haven't you? I remember you telling me that you had it when you were very young.

Laurie Yes, why should you . . .

Jo It's Beth; we think she's caught it and we don't want to take any chances of passing it on.

Laurie Oh, I am sorry. What can I do to help?

Jo Nothing at the moment, but if it is as bad as we fear, Amy must go to stay with Aunt March until Beth is better. Meg is out in the kitchen breaking the news to her now, but if I know Amy, Meg won't have an easy task, for Aunt March petrifies her. Laurie, Amy thinks a lot of you and takes notice of what you say. Try to make her see that it is only for her own good if we have to send her away.

Laurie Well, I'll try to do what . . .

Jo There's my good boy! (*She moves to the stairs*) Now I must go up and help Hannah; you wait here in case you're needed.

She moves up the stairs, but pauses to indicate that his diplomacy is needed at once, for Amy bursts into the room in a great rage, and with a somewhat exasperated Meg in tow

Amy (*as she enters*) No, Meg, no! I'd rather have the fever ten times over than go to Aunt March!

Meg But, my dear, if Beth is really ill we shall be busy nursing her, and it would be no help to anyone if you are sick too.

Amy I don't wish to be sent off as if I was in the way! Besides it's always so horrid at Aunt March's with her rules and orders and "things-to-do" and lectures on "how-one-should behave". I should have to do all the things Jo does—like feeding that awful parrot. It always screams at me when I go near it and pecks at my hair. And I cannot endure her fat, cross, little beast of a dog either, for it snarls and yelps whenever it sees me. And the cook is so bad-tempered I dare not go near the kitchen, and the coachman is deaf, and the . . .

Laurie Whoa! There is no need to go on and on and on! We gather that you don't greatly relish a stay with your Aunt March; but you must be a sensible little woman and do as the others say. You don't *want* to be sick, do you?

Amy No, I'm sure I don't; but I dare say I shall be, for I've been with Beth all the time.

Laurie That's the very reason you ought to go away at once, so that you may escape it. Change of air will keep you well. I advise you to be off as soon as you can for scarlet fever is no joke, miss.

Amy But everything is so grim at Aunt March's. It's just like Orphans in the Underworld!

During the next speech Jo appears on the stairs. She stops to listen and remains still throughout the ensuing dialogue

Laurie I'll tell you what I'll do. If you go to Aunt March's I'll come every day and take you out driving or walking. Now, it wouldn't be so grim, would it, with me popping in to tell you how Beth is, and to take you out gallivanting? The old lady likes me, and I'll be as sweet as possible to her to make things easy for you.

Amy (*considering the proposition*) Will you take me out in the trotting-wagon with the new pony?

Laurie On my honour as a gentleman.

Amy And come every single day?

Laurie See if I don't.

Amy And bring me back the minute Beth is well?

Laurie The identical minute.

Amy And, perhaps—take me to the theatre?

Laurie A dozen theatres if necessary.

Amy (*slowly and somewhat reluctantly*) Well—all right then—if Beth is really ill, then I'll go.

Laurie Good girl!

Meg (*with relief*) Oh, thank you, Laurie! Now, Amy, I'm going to get the doctor at once. I think the sooner Beth is under his care the better. Aunt March will be here shortly, so just be a good girl, and do as you are asked.

Meg moves into the hall, takes her bonnet and cloak from the hallstand and pulls them on as she goes out of the front door

Jo descends the last few stairs and enters the room

Jo (*moving in as Meg goes out*) Thank you, Laurie, you're a real trump.

Laurie How is Beth?

Jo I think she feels a little better now that she is lying down. The baby's death has upset her a good deal, poor dear. (*Rumpling her hair*) Oh, what a trying world it is! No sooner do we get out of one trouble than down comes another. There doesn't seem to be anything to hold on to when Mother's not here, so I'm all at sea.

Laurie (*trying to cheer her up*) Well, haul in your tops'l, Jo, and tell me if I should telegraph to her.

Jo That's what troubles me. I think we *ought* to tell her if Beth is really ill, but Hannah says we mustn't, for Mother can't leave Father just yet, and it

would only make them anxious. Mother told us that we were to mind
what Hannah said, so I suppose we must, but it doesn't seem quite right
to me.

Laurie Hmm, well, I don't know what to say. Suppose you ask Grandfather
after the doctor has been?

Jo Yes, that seems the sensible thing to do. Laurie, be a dear, and do one
more good turn for us today.

Laurie (*with a theatrical flourish*) Yours to command, ma'am!

Jo Stay and play up to Aunt March a little when she arrives—so that she'll
be sweeter about having Amy. (*Turning to Amy*) Amy, I'm going upstairs
to pack a few things for you so that you'll be ready to go back with Aunt
March if it's necessary. (*She moves to the stairs, but stops to turn back in
the archway*) Remember your promise now, Amy!

Jo exits briskly upstairs

*Amy is more than a little affronted by this second admonishment. With an air
of martyred resignation she crosses to the bookcase*

Amy Well, everyone seems to have made up their mind that I shall have to
go and stay with Aunt March. If I *do* have to one never knows what might
happen to me there, so I think I had better give you my will—just in case.

Laurie (*unprepared for this trust*) Your what?

Amy (*turning from the bookcase as she pulls out her drawing portfolio*) My
will. My last will and testament. I drew it up a while ago and put it into
my drawing-book for safe-keeping. (*She takes out a folded paper which she
hands to Laurie*)

Laurie Do you think this is really necessary, Amy?

Amy (*with a great sense of tragedy*) I want to be ready. Life is uncertain, and
I don't want any ill-feeling over my tomb.

Laurie But why give it to me?

Amy I want you to read it through to see if it is legal and right, and then to
witness it for me.

Laurie (*suppressing his amusement as he unfolds the paper; reading*) "I, Amy
Curtis March, being in my sane mind, and in, full possession of all my
senses, do hereby and from henceforth give and bequeath all my earthly
property—viz., to wit—namely—"

Amy (*her sense of propriety intervening*) I don't think that it should be read
aloud until after I am dead.

Laurie (*absorbed*) What? Oh, sorry! (*He continues reading to himself with
some expressions of surprise at the contents*)

These reactions are not entirely pleasing to Amy

(*Suddenly he reads aloud again*) "To my sister, Margaret, I leave my
turquoise ring" . . . er . . . are you *sure* you spell turquoise with a "k"?

Amy (*snatching the will from him with some irritation*) I wouldn't have
shown it to you if I'd thought you were going to pick it full of holes!
(*Tragic again*) You'll be sorry after I'm gone! I suppose all that is
necessary is for you to witness my signature. (*Turning to the document*

with renewed solemnity) "And now having disposed of my most valuable property, I hope all will be satisfied and not blame the dead. I forgive everyone, and trust we may all meet when the last trump shall sound. Amen." (*She pauses, slightly overcome by her own eloquence*) "To this will and testament I set my hand and seal on this twentieth day of November, Annie Domino Eighteen-sixty-one." (*She takes up a pen, and writes*) "Amy Curtis March." (*Passing it to Laurie*) Now, Laurie, just sign your name below mine.

Laurie obediently complies

Don't people sometimes put sort of postscripts to their wills?
Laurie Yes. "Codicils", they call them.
Amy (*making the final sacrifice*) Put one to mine, then—that I wish all my curls to be cut off, and given around to my friends. I forgot it; but I want it done—though it will spoil my looks.

As Laurie adds this request ...

Aunt March appears in the archway, having overheard this last speech

Aunt March What's that I hear? You're going to have all your hair cut off—like that muddle-headed sister of yours! Merciful Heavens, if this sort of thing continues it won't be long before this house looks like a convict settlement!
Laurie (*rising*) I'm sorry, ma'am, we didn't hear you ring.
Aunt March Ring, young man! What is the purpose of my ringing, I should like to know! If there is sickness in the house then there is no point in setting up a great jangle of bells every five minutes! I just walked straight in!

Jo appears on the stairs, and enters the room. She carries Amy's cloak and bonnet, and a small portmanteau which she sets down

Jo Oh, Aunt March, thank goodness you've come.
Aunt March I've just seen your sister Meg. She came jumping around in front of the carriage to attract my attention like a demented dervish. Frightened the coachman out of his wits! I wonder the horses didn't bolt. Just going off for the doctor she tells me. What's all this about Beth being laid up with the scarlet fever?
Jo We are not sure, Aunt March, but we think she may have caught it.
Aunt March (*moving to a chair*) Humph! Wouldn't surprise me if she has! What else can you expect if you *will* go poking about among poor folks? I was always telling your mother the same thing—though I might just as well have saved my breath! Well, Master Laurence and what are you doing here? And Amy, moping about as usual, I see!
Jo We are worried about Amy; you see, she hasn't had the fever and—well—we wondered if she might come and stay with you till it's all over.

There is a pause while Aunt March considers this unexpected proposition, and glances darkly at the increasingly disheartened Amy who now begins to weep softly

Amy begins to weep softly

Aunt March Mmm, well, I suppose she can come and stay—providing she makes herself useful and as long as she isn't sick, though I have no doubt she will be—she certainly looks like it. Don't snivel, child, it irritates me to hear people making that noise.

Jo Oh, thank you, Aunt March, it's kind of you and it will be such a relief to know . . .

Aunt March You'll be wanted here to help nurse and look after your sister; so Amy will be able to take on your tasks. And I'm not at all sure that she won't do them a great deal better, I know for a fact that my sweet Polly and Mop, my doggie, are quite devoted to her.

Amy (*reacting to this astonishing piece of news*) But, Aunt March, they always . . .

Aunt March (*cutting her short as she turns to address Jo*) What do you hear from your mother?

Jo Father is much better, I'm glad to say.

Aunt March Oh, is he? Well, that won't last long, I fancy: March never had any stamina. Now that your mother's gone chasing off to Washington as well, it would never surprise me if they both . . .

Laurie (*stepping in diplomatically*) I hope you will have no objection, ma'am, if I come over to visit Amy each day whilst she is staying with you. We could go driving for an hour or so, and I would be able to give her news of Beth and the . . .

Aunt March Mercy on me! We have it all arranged, haven't we? I am not at all sure that it would be quite proper for her to be gadding about with a rattle-pated boy whilst she is in my care. (*Darkly*) What goes on here is, of course, another matter, but if she is to be . . .

Mercifully, at this point Hannah appears on the stairs, and, descending swiftly, enters the room

Hannah I don't think there's any doubt that Miss Beth has the scarlatina, mum. I've seen them symptoms afore. I reckon the sooner Miss Amy's out of this house the better—just to be on the safe side. Now, I must go and get some warm water to bathe that poor babby upstairs.

Hannah exits quickly to the kitchen

Jo helps the unwilling Amy into her cloak and bonnet as Laurie takes up the bag

Jo I hope it won't inconvenience you too greatly, Aunt March. I'm sorry if . . .

Aunt March (*rising*) It seems to me that everything was very neatly planned long before I arrived. So, let us not discuss, Miss, what is or is not convenient to me! (*To Jo, more quietly so that the others shall not hear*) See that Beth has everything she needs—and you may tell the doctor to send his bill to me. (*Turning to survey the unhappy Amy*) Well, child! Are you coming or not? We have not all day to waste, you know, and there is much to be done at home. Sunday may be a day of rest, but we do not give ourselves over entirely to pleasure-seeking and self-indulgence! (*She moves up to the archway*)

Amy (*to the others, miserably*) I don't think I'll be able to bear it—but I'll try!

Aunt March (*turning in the archway to see if Amy is following*) Merciful heavens! What a cheerless object! Anyone would think you were going to your execution!

Aunt March sweeps out

Amy begins to follow, but in the archway she turns despondently to the others

Amy I feel as though I am!

She exits forlornly as ...

The Lights fade to Black-out

SCENE 2

The same. Ten days later. Late evening

When the Lights come up the parlour is empty, lit only by the lamplight from the hall

After a moment Jo descends the stairs slowly. Half-way down she pauses and looks back as if half-expecting to be called. She reaches the hall, pauses again looking up the stairs, and moves into the parlour. Her movements are restless, and she is obviously ill at ease. She turns up the lamp by Marmee's chair, and we can see by the light of it that she is tired and very drawn. She crosses and turns up the lamp on the C table; her eye falls on Beth's little piano, now closed and locked, and she moves over to caress the lid gently. For a moment she stands looking down at it

The sound of the front door opening makes her turn abruptly

Meg enters in a bonnet and cloak, and as she moves into the light we see that she, too, has a heavy, tired look in her eyes

Meg (*as she removes her bonnet*) Is the doctor here, Jo?

Jo Yes, he's upstairs now. He told me to come down and rest while he examined Beth. How can I rest when she's up there ...? (*She gives a gesture of despair*) Oh, Meg! Why doesn't he do something to make her better?

Meg (*moving to her*) He's been doing all he can do, Jo; and now he's coming in twice a day. We can't expect any more, and you can't go on like this, you'll be ill yourself. You've hardly closed your eyes for three days now.

Jo But, Meg, I can't leave her now! While you've been out she's been worse—tossing about, talking in that hoarse, broken voice, even trying to sing. Her little hands playing on the coverlet as if it were her beloved piano. If only she knew us when we spoke to her! Worst of all, she keeps on calling out imploringly for Marmee.

Meg I can't help feeling that we ought to have sent for Mother, but Hannah has been so adamant about not worrying her or Father.

Jo (*trying to pull herself together*) How dark the days seem now, and the house seems even sadder and lonelier than ever!

Meg It's bitterly cold outside. I think we shall have snow later tonight. I mailed the letter to Mother, but I feel so guilty writing to her as if nothing were wrong and not mentioning Beth's illness.

During the next speech Hannah descends the stairs slowly and moves into the room. Her face is troubled and there is something in her expression that immediately catches the girls' attention

Jo Oh, Meg, it doesn't seem so long ago that we were complaining about every little hardship, and now here we are with so much that we hold dear hanging in the balance.

Meg (*rising*) Hannah! What is it?

Hannah (*fighting to keep her emotions in check*) The doctor ... the doctor thinks your Ma should be sent for.

Jo (*with a quick look at Meg*) She isn't ...? She can't be ...

Hannah The poor little lamb's about as ill as she can be. She seems to have taken a turn for the worse today. The doctor ain't sure just how things may go, but he says he reckons she'll reach a crisis within the next hour or so.

Jo (*with a desperate impatience*) We must *do* something ... We can't just sit here and ...

Hannah (*quietly*) I guess there ain't nothing we *can* do until that crisis comes. It's a kind of battle she has to fight all by herself. The doctor's given her some sort of powder, and wants to sit with her awhile until it takes effect. I've just come down for that telegram we wrote out ready to send to your Ma ... if it was needed. (*She moves to the mantelpiece and picks up a folded paper*) The doctor's said he'll drop it into the telegraph office on his way home. (*She is very near to tears as she turns to leave the room*) He thought it would save us a journey on a cold night. (*At the archway she pauses and turns back to the others in a sudden moment of defeat*) I ... I ... I guess I was wrong ... I'm sorry, my dears. We should have sent for your Ma awhile ago, when you wanted to, but I thought your Pa needed her nursing as long as possible, and ... I thought ... now, maybe, I've left it too late ... I ... I don't know ... I ... (*The tears well up. She smothers her sobs in the hem of her apron*)

Meg (*moving to her*) Hannah, dear, don't. You did what you thought best. Come, let's go up and see if the doctor needs anything.

They move to the stairs

Jo If life is often as hard as this, I don't see how we shall ever get through it.

Hannah moves upstairs

Meg (*turning in the archway*) I wish I hadn't a heart, mine aches too much.

She turns and follows Hannah

Jo (*sinking onto the stool by the piano*) If God spares Beth I will never complain again—ever. I promise!

The front door is heard to open

Laurie enters the parlour quietly, looking up the stairs at Meg and Hannah as they disappear

Laurie Hallo, Jo. What's the news? I saw the doctor arrive earlier, but I couldn't wait any longer.
Jo The doctor's told us to send for Mother.
Laurie It's not as bad as that, is it?
Jo Yes, it is, Laurie. (*Tears start to fall*) She doesn't know us, she doesn't even look like my Beth any more—and there's nobody to help us bear it; Mother and Father aren't here, and God seems so far away that I can't find Him.

As Jo reaches the end of her speech she breaks down completely, her hand stretching out helplessly as if groping in the dark. Tenderly Laurie takes it; for a moment he hesitates, then with a look of deep compassion, he folds her in his arms

Laurie I'm here, Jo. Hold on to me.

For a moment or two Jo sobs in his arms. Laurie strokes her hair gently, and rests his head against hers in an endeavour to comfort her. Jo pulls out her handkerchief

Jo (*breaking away from him as she dries her eyes*) Thank you, Laurie. I'm—I'm better now. I don't feel so forlorn and I'll try to bear whatever comes.
Laurie Keep hoping for the best; that will help you, Jo. Poor girl, you're worn out. It isn't like you to be forlorn. (*A sudden idea occurs to him*) Stop a bit! I know just the thing to hearten you in a jiffy! (*He moves up to the bookcase, takes out a bottle of wine and two glasses and pours wine for them both*) A sip of wine will warm you up and cheer you up, and soon your mother will be here, and then everything will be all right!
Jo (*cheering up under Laurie's lively influence*) I am so glad that Father is better. Marmee won't feel so bad about leaving him, for he is not yet well enough to make the journey himself. Oh, me! It does seem as if all the troubles come in a heap. But to have Marmee home again will be wonderful!
Laurie (*bringing the glasses to her*) There you are! Now drink it up—it will help, I'm sure!
Jo Thank you. Let's drink health and a swift recovery to Beth.
Jo
Laurie } (*together*) To Beth!
Jo You are a good doctor, Laurie, and *such* a comfortable friend.
Laurie (*with a note of suppressed excitement in his voice*) Thank you for those few kind words, but I haven't finished my treatment yet! I have

something to tell you that is going to warm the cockles of your heart better than quarts of wine!

Jo What is it?

Laurie (*triumphantly*) I telegraphed to your mother yesterday, and Brooke answered that she'd come at once. She'll be here tonight! Now! Perhaps within the next ten minutes or so if her train is on time! It was due on the hour and Grandpa has gone to the station to meet her with the carriage while I came to break the news to you. (*He pauses*)

For the moment, Jo can make no reply

Aren't you glad that I did it?

Jo (*leaping up and throwing her arms around Laurie*) Oh, Laurie! Laurie! Here tonight, just when we need her most! Oh, I am so glad! (*She laughs almost hysterically and clings to Laurie*)

For the moment he is somewhat overcome, but recovering himself he pats her soothingly and follows this up with a bashful kiss or two. This brings Jo back to reality at once, and she pulls away from him

Goodness! I'm sorry, I didn't mean to do that; it was dreadful of me, but I was so thrilled by your news. You are such a dear to have brought about the answer to my prayers that I couldn't help flying at you. Tell me about it (*she hands him her half-emptied glass*) and I don't think I had better have any more of that wine; it makes me act so stupidly.

Laurie (*laughing and putting his tie straight*) It didn't seem stupid to me! I didn't mind one little bit! (*He becomes serious again*) You see Grandpa and I got very uneasy, for Beth seemed no better. We thought that your mother ought to know. She'd never forgive us if Beth—well, if anything happened, you know. So yesterday I got Grandpa to say it was high time we did something, and off I went and telegraphed to Washington.

Jo Laurie, you're an angel! How shall I ever thank you?

Laurie (*with a mischievous grin*) Well, you could fly at me once again. I rather liked it!

Jo Now, Laurie, that will do! I'll do it by proxy, when your Grandpa comes!

Meg appears on the stairs and comes swiftly down

(*Turning joyously to her*) Oh, Meg! Isn't it wonderful! Laurie and Mr Laurence had already sent for Marmee! She'll be here at any minute; she is coming ... (*She breaks off, arrested by the grave expression on Meg's face*) Meg, what is it? What's happened? Is she ...?

Meg crosses nervously to sit in the chair by the fire

Meg (*quietly, in a frightened voice*) I don't know ... I ... I can't tell. Hannah and I were talking quietly by the fire when we heard a sound from the bed—it was almost like a little sigh; we went over and Beth ... (*She falters, uncertain of what she must say*)

Jo Yes, Meg, yes?

Meg That feverish flush and look of pain had gone. Her little face looked so pale and peaceful—a sort of utter repose. (*She looks at Jo*) Then I got frightened, I couldn't stay—I had to come down.

Jo Oh, Meg! (*She turns as if to make for the stairs*)

Hannah appears on the stairs and hastens down

All three look at her expectantly

She is breathless—partly with the exertion of hurrying and partly with excitement. For a moment she pauses by the archway to catch her breath. Her expression, conveying neither grief nor joy, gives them no clue to what may have happened. Her voice is strained and, at first, she has difficulty in getting her words out

Hannah It's ... it's over. I ... I can hardly believe it's happened ... the fever's turned. (*Her voice gains strength*) She's sleepin' natural! Her skin's damp and she's breathin' easy. Praise be given ... she's going to be all right! (*She buries her face in her apron for a moment, and, then, briskly wipes away the tears and turns back to the stairs*) I must go back, but I had to tell you that she's going to be all right!

Hannah exits hurriedly upstairs

The girls hug each other in ecstasy. Laurie moves to the window and draws the curtain aside

Outside the snow is falling quite fast

Meg (*halfway between joy and tears*) And when she wakes Mother will be here to greet her.

Jo (*catching the sound, muffled in the snow, of a carriage arriving*) Listen! It's the carriage!

Laurie (*turning from the window, his voice jubilant*) She's here! She's home again!

The Lights fade quickly to Black-out

SCENE 3

The same. A few weeks later. Christmas morning about noon

Winter sunshine streams through the window to brighten every corner of the room which is again decorated for the festive season with evergreens and vases of holly and winter flowers. A Christmas tree, with all its glittering trimmings, stands once more in the window

We hear a carol begin softly in the Black-out, rising to full strength as the Lights come up

When the Lights come up Marmee, seated at the piano, is leading a vigorous final chorus of "Ding-Dong Merrily on High!" which Meg, Jo and Amy, grouped in the archway, are singing loudly and lustily for the benefit of Beth who is upstairs in bed. As it ends with a triumphant shout, there is a burst of mutual praise and laughter from everyone. It is obvious that this is an item in a small concert of carols for the convalescent Beth. The singers, though a trifle breathless, seem keen to continue. They all speak at once

Meg Mother, do let's sing *Whilst Shepherds Watched*!

Jo No, Meg, no! We must have *Good King Wenceslas*! Marmee, please!

Amy What about *We Three Kings From Orient Are*? It's my favourite! Oh, please!

Marmee (*rising as she waves away these entreaties with a smile*) No, no, no, girls! No more now, we'll sing again later! We have given Beth a little concert of carols for Christmas morning, and, now, we must think about Christmas dinner—or Mr Laurence and Laurie will be here before we are ready for them!

Hannah enters with a tray of eight punch glasses which she sets down on the table

Hannah That's a fine fat turkey that the old gentleman sent in, and no mistake! Roasting nicely, it is. I've brought the glasses, mum, but they need a'polishin'. I'll bring the fruit punch as soon as it's ready.

Marmee Thank you, Hannah. Jo and I will do the glasses.

The front door bell rings

Goodness! Our guests are here already! Amy, dear, do let them in, and then go up and help Beth

Amy exits quickly to the front door

In the hall we hear the exchange of Christmas greetings between Amy, Mr Laurence and Laurie, and Amy explaining that she is going up to Beth

Amy mounts the stairs

Mr Laurence and Laurie appear in the archway

Meanwhile, Marmee has been hastily organizing the rest of her household

(*Continuing as Amy exits*) Meg, I am sure that Hannah could do with some help in the kitchen.

Meg (*immediately turning to go*) Of course, Mother. Shall I give you a hand with the fruit punch, Hannah?

Meg and Hannah move upstage, exchanging Christmas greetings with the Laurences as they exit to the kitchen. Hannah bobs a curtsey to Mr Laurence

Marmee Jo, perhaps you will help here? (*She turns to greet the guests as they enter*) Come in, Mr Laurence! Laurie! A very happy Christmas to you both! And thank you for the many gifts you sent over this morning.

Mr Laurence (*waving aside her thanks as he warmly shakes her hand*) My pleasure, ma'am, I do assure you! The compliments of the season to you, ma'am! (*Turning to Jo*) And to you, too, young woman!

Laurie Happy Christmas to you, Mrs March! Happy Christmas, Jo!

Surprising everyone with a mock formal bow, Jo clears her throat impressively and produces, with one of her best theatrical flourishes, a small scroll which she unrolls

Jo Special "pome" for the Festive Season! (*She turns to Mr Laurence and Laurie*)
> God bless you, jolly gentlemen!
> May nothing you dismay,
> But health and peace and happiness
> Be yours, this Christmas Day!

She bows again amid laughter and applause from the others

Mr Laurence 'Pon my soul! Poems *and* carols! We could hear you singing before we left the house! Most welcoming for your guests!

Marmee (*laughing*) The carols were meant only for Beth's ears!

Mr Laurence How is our little convalescent?

Marmee Improving daily. She stayed in bed this morning so that she might feel strong enough to join us for Christmas dinner, but, now that she knows you are here, I am sure she will want to come down at once!

Mr Laurence May we, perhaps, go up to her?

Marmee She would be delighted, and, perhaps, you and Laurie would be kind enough to bring her down?

Laurie (*leading the way to the stairs*) We specialize in conveying pretty invalids!

Mr Laurence (*as he follows Laurie*) We will take the greatest care, ma'am.

Laurie and Mr Laurence exit upstairs

Marmee I know she couldn't be in safer hands. (*She turns back to Jo, and moves to the tray of glasses*) Come, Jo, we must get these glasses polished. (*She takes up a glass and a napkin from the tray and starts polishing*)

Jo crosses to join her, and taking up a second glass and napkin follows Marmee's example. Throughout the conversation which follows they continue to work until the task is done

Jo With Laurie and Mr Laurence here, it's going to be a real family dinner, isn't it, Marmee? If only Father had been well enough to come home it would have been absolutely perfect.

Marmee In his last letter he speaks hopefully of coming early in the new year. (*She looks towards the window*) And now the weather has turned so mild it will encourage him. So, we shall have that to look forward to.

Jo (*frowning slightly*) I suppose Mr Brooke will be coming with him.

Marmee (*surprised at this sudden change of thought*) But, of course, dear, why not? He stayed to nurse your father where I had to leave off, and would not dream of letting him make the journey alone.

Jo I know and I am grateful to him, Marmee, for what he has done, but . . .

Marmee (*understanding*) But, what, dearie? Is it about Meg?

Jo How quickly you guessed! Oh, Mother, I *am* so worried. It all started last New Year's Eve. She lost a glove that evening and although Laurie searched everywhere, it was never found. And do you know what had happened to it, Marmee?

Marmee I might guess, but you tell me, Jo.

Jo Mr Brooke had picked it up and carried it around in his pocket! Laurie told me that it fell out with some papers one day when he was at lessons with Mr Brooke. Of course, Laurie joked him about it, and he owned that he liked Meg, but didn't dare say so as he had so little money and but few prospects.

Marmee (*thoughtfully*) I see.

Jo When he went away I hoped that might put an end to it all, but of course, if he's coming back ... (*Despondently*) Isn't it a *dreadful* state of things?

Marmee Do you think Meg cares for him?

Jo Christopher Columbus! I don't know anything about love and such nonsense! In novels, the girls show it by starting and blushing, fainting away, growing thin, and generally acting like fools. But Meg doesn't do anything of that sort.

Marmee Then you fancy that Meg is not interested in John?

Jo Who?

Marmee Mr Brooke. I call him John now; we fell into the way of doing so at the hospital and he likes it.

Jo (*dismally*) Oh, dear! I know you'll take his part. He's been good to Father, and you won't send him away, but let Meg marry him if she wants to.

Marmee Now, my dear, don't get hot-headed about it. He was perfectly open and honourable about Meg, for he told us that he loved her, but that he would earn enough to give her a comfortable home before he asked her to marry him.

Jo I knew there was mischief brewing! I felt it! But it's far worse than I imagined. I just wish I could marry Meg myself, and keep her safe in the family.

Marmee When John comes back, and I see them together, I shall be able to judge her feelings towards him.

Jo Oh, she'll look into those handsome brown eyes she's always talking about, and then it will be all up with her. She'll go and fall in love and that will be an end of peace and fun and good times together. I can see it all! They'll go lovering around the house and we shall have to dodge them. Oh, dear me! Why weren't we all boys—then there wouldn't be any bother!

Marmee If it is any comfort to you, Jo, your father and I have agreed that Meg shall not commit herself in any way for a year or two. She is young, and if she and John love one another, they can wait, and test that love by doing so.

Jo But, Marmee, wouldn't you rather she married a rich man?

Marmee You know my views on that, my dear; I am content to see Meg begin humbly, for, if I am not mistaken, she will be rich in the possession of a good man's heart and that is better than any fortune.

Jo I suppose you're right, but I'm disappointed about Meg for I'd planned to have her marry Laurie by and by, and sit in the lap of luxury all her days. Wouldn't that be nice?

Marmee (*laughing kindly*) Don't make plans for others, Jo. Let time and their own hearts guide your friends—*and* your sisters.

Jo But Laurie's rich and generous and good, and loves us all; and *I* say it's a great pity my plan is spoilt! Oh dear! I wish wearing flat-irons on our heads would keep us from growing up. But buds bloom into roses, I suppose, and kittens grow into cats—more's the pity!

Meg enters

Meg (*hearing the last few lines*) What's that about flat-irons and cats?

Jo Oh, nothing—just some of my nonsense. Does Hannah need any more help?

Meg No, it's all done now, thank you, Jo.

The sound of laughter and chatter on the stairs attracts their attention

Down the stairs, preceded by Laurie, and followed by Amy, comes Mr Laurence carrying Beth. She is looking paler than when last we saw her, and a little thinner, but her eyes are bright and she is smiling happily. She is dressed, but wrapped in a warm rug

Marmee Ah, here is the rest of our party! (*She moves to the sofa where, helped by Meg, cushions are plumped up and arranged to receive the small invalid*)

Meg follows Marmee

As the others enter the parlour, Hannah reappears to join in the general welcome and jubilation. During the following dialogue, whilst Marmee, Hannah and Mr Laurence settle Beth on the sofa, Jo beckons Meg, Amy and Laurie to the fire where they whisper together in a somewhat hilarious conspiracy

You are looking so much better today, Beth, dear. Are you sure you are warm enough?

Mr Laurence Are you comfortable, my dear?

Beth (*sighing happily*) Oh, yes, thank you. It's just so lovely to be down here with everyone. After the carols, I was afraid you might forget me!

Marmee As if we could ever do that!

Hannah Land sakes! You're never out of our thoughts!

Beth Oh, Marmee, I'm so full of happiness that I don't think I could hold one drop more!

The conspirators emerge suddenly from their huddle, and approach the invalid. Jo steps forward as spokesman

Jo (*her histrionic talents again taking over*) Dear Queen Bess! As the fairest turtle-dove in this family of partridges, we dedicate this ancient madrigal to you!

She turns to the others, and, with a great flourish, leads them into a spirited version of "The Twelve Days of Christmas". Once the singing has started, they join hands to dance in an uncompleted ring around the sofa. Marmee and Mr Laurence draw to one side to allow the dancers freedom, but enter into the spirit of it all by joining in the singing—as does Hannah, though she is unprepared when she is suddenly grabbed by Jo and Laurie and drawn, protestingly, into the dance on the second verse. The volume and activity increase. Beth sits up delightedly, clapping her hands in time with the song

The third verse has just commenced with enormous vigour when a figure in a long cloak and muffler appears in the archway. It is John Brooke

The singing and dancing stop suddenly. There is a silence as everyone's eyes turn towards him. For a moment longer no one speaks

Meg (*involuntarily, her voice breaking the silence*) Why, John! (*Confused*) I mean ... Mr Brooke!

Mr Laurence Bless my soul! It's Brooke! What are you doing here, man?

Brooke is a little embarrassed at being the subject of quite so much attention

Brooke (*with an air of suppressed excitment and a smile on his lips*) I ... I'm sorry to interrupt, but I ... I've got a special Christmas present for the March family! (*He steps back*)

A second figure appears in the archway. It is that of a man of middle years whose strength of character and kindly disposition show clearly in a face that has recently known ill-health. He has about him the tired air of one who has made a long journey, but his face lights up at the scene before him. He has loosened his long cloak and muffler to reveal the dark clothes of a minister of religion. Mr March has come home. There is another brief silence—this time of disbelief—before he speaks

Mr March (*with a smile*) Am I in time for Christmas dinner?

From silence the room erupts into an uproar of welcome. Everyone speaks at once

Jo rushes forward with Marmee to embrace him and draw him into the parlour

Jo Father! Father! You're home! Christopher Columbus! What a marvellous present!

There is a general confusion of greeting and exclamations of surprise and delight as Mr March is enveloped in three pairs of loving arms by his daughters. The air is full of: "I just can't believe it!" "How did you get here?", "When did you arrive?", "How are you feeling, Father?", "What a lovely surprise!", "This makes it just the happiest Christmas ever!", etc.

Meanwhile, Mr Laurence and Laurie are greeting Brooke and welcoming him home. He has now removed his cloak and muffler, and is seen to be wearing army lieutenant's uniform. Mr March, divested of his cloak and muffler by Marmee and the girls, now breaks away from the others to go to the little figure on the sofa who sits up holding out her arms to him imploringly. He sits on the sofa, holding her in his arms

Mr March I can hardly believe that I am really home again! I've often thought how much I should like to arrive and surprise you all on Christmas day, but it seemed a very remote possibility. When the weather turned finer a few days ago, the doctor thought I may take advantage of it and make the journey. So, we made some hurried arrangements, and here we are!

Marmee It makes it just the happiest Christmas we could hope for, doesn't it girls?

There is loud and lively agreement from the girls

Mr March Well, you may thank John for really bringing it about.

Brooke Oh, I don't know, sir, I did . . .

Mr March Oh, yes, John. I could never have made the journey alone. It is due entirely to your efforts that we are here now. (*To the others*) I don't know what I would have done without him in these last few months for he has been devoted to me. (*Turning again to Brooke*) You won't like hearing me say it, I know, but you are altogether a most estimable young man.

This glowing tribute embarrasses the recipient, who hardly knows where to look, and is received with totally contrasting reactions by Meg and Jo

Marmee That is true indeed! We owe you a great debt of gratitude, John.

Conscious of Brooke's embarrassment, Marmee changes the subject to more practical matters

Well now, you must both be famished after your journey. Dinner is nearly ready and I . . .

Hannah, who has taken her part, alternating between tears and laughter, in the general rejoicing at the return of Mr March, is suddenly brought back to reality by the word "dinner". She lets out a loud cry

Hannah Land sakes, mum! The turkey! I must get back and baste him before he dies of thirst in the oven!

Hannah exits speedily to the kitchen

The others laugh

Beth Marmee, please, I always help to baste the turkey, and this is such a *special* Christmas that I'd hate to miss doing it.

Marmee (*uncertainly*) Well, I don't know . . . you must take things quietly for a little while, and let *us* wait on you . . .

Mr March (*seeing the disappointment on Beth's face*) Oh, I don't suppose that small task will be too exhausting! (*He takes Beth in his arms and rises*) We'll all go! Beth can sit in Hannah's rocking-chair by the fire and superintend everything. (*Rallying the others he moves upstage with Beth*)

Amy rushes ahead to tell Hannah

Come, Mr Laurence, Laurie, John—join us! That turkey's in for the basting of its life!

There is a ripple of laughter from the others as they follow him and exit to the kitchen

Brooke, the last to move, suddenly realizes that he is still holding his hat, cloak, muffler and gloves. He looks about for somewhere to put them. Seeing this, Meg moves up and takes them from him

For a moment, a look lingers between them, then Brooke exits to the kitchen

Meg looks down at the hat and garments in her arms with something rather close to affection before she turns and moves to hang them on the hallstand, beyond our view, near the front door

This brief scene, not lost on Jo who has been busily engaged in gathering up her father's things—scattered in the tumult of his arrival—has not escaped Marmee's eyes either

Marmee (*as Meg crosses to the hallstand*) I must go to the dining-room, and lay two more places! (*She moves upstage, but, as Meg passes out of sight, turns back to Jo, and lowers her voice*) Jo, dear, I think you will have to resign yourself to the fact that, if Meg does not love John already, I have a feeling that she will very soon learn to!

Marmee turns again and exits briskly to the dining-room

As she does so, Laurie enters from the kitchen

Laurie (*in the archway*) Come on, Jo! Aren't you going to join us?
Jo (*grimly*) There won't be room for all of us in the kitchen. I'll tidy up in here—and, anyway, right now I *hate* estimable young men with handsome brown eyes! (*She proceeds to vent some of her spleen on the innocent sofa cushions*)

Laurie shrugs and returns to the kitchen as ...

Meg enters and moves slowly to the fire. Her mood is decidedly romantic

Jo eyes her balefully for a moment or two whilst she struggles to allow something of the spirit of Christmas to overcome her less generous thoughts

Jo (*grudgingly*) Well, I suppose we must be grateful to *your* John for getting Father home for Christmas.
Meg (*her reverie rudely broken into*) Don't call him "my John", it isn't proper and it doesn't happen to be true.
Jo You certainly act as though you would rather like it to be. It was nauseating the way you were looking at each other just now.
Meg (*with a touch of annoyance*) Oh, really, Jo!
Jo I'm sorry, I don't mean to plague you, Meg; but I do hate all this

uncertainty. If you mean to accept him, then, for goodness sake, make haste, and let us have it over and done with!

Meg I can't say or do anything until he speaks, now can I?

Jo If he did speak you wouldn't know what to say, you'd cry or blush or give in to him, instead of giving a good decided "No".

Meg I'm not so silly and weak as you think. I know just what I should say, for I've planned it all so that I needn't be taken unawares. There's no knowing what may happen, and I wish to be prepared.

Jo Would you mind telling me just what you'd say?

Meg Not at all, for my experience may be useful to you, by and by, in your own affairs of this sort.

Jo Don't mean to have any! It's bad enough to have to watch other people, but I should feel a prize fool doing it myself.

Meg I think not, if you liked someone very much—and he liked you. (*She pauses, lost for a moment in happy reflection*)

Jo (*bringing her back to reality*) I thought you were going to tell me what you had in mind to say to that man.

Meg I should merely say, quite calmly and decidedly, "Thank you, Mr Brooke, you are very kind, but I agree with Father that I should not enter into any engagement just at present; so please say no more, but let us be friends as we were."

Jo (*unconvinced*) Hmm! Well, that's stiff and cool enough; but I don't believe that you'll ever say it—and I know he wouldn't accept it if you did. He'll go on like one of those rejected lovers in books and you'll give in rather than hurt his feelings.

Meg (*anxious to prove that she is not as weak-willed as her sister imagines*) No, I won't! I shall tell him I've made up my mind, and walk out of the room with dignity. (*She turns to demonstrate this proposed exercise, and comes face to face with . . .*)

Brooke, who appears suddenly in the archway

Oh, Mr Brooke! I . . . er . . . I . . . do come in and sit down. (*She turns back into the room in confusion*)

Brooke Thank you. I hope I don't intrude?

Jo Not at all, Mr Brooke. (*She looks pointedly at Meg*) You've come at just the right moment! I must go and help Marmee in the dining-room, but I am sure Meg will be glad of your company! (*She moves into the archway and turns back*)

Brooke has his back to Jo, so she is able to signal freely to Meg that she should put her plan into action. Brooke, conscious that something has taken Meg's eye over his shoulder, turns to discover what it may be

Jo, caught out, strives to turn her gestures into a convincing, if rather self-conscious, wave of farewell as she exits hurriedly to the dining-room

Brooke turns back to Meg with a smile. There is an awkward pause

Meg (*in sudden panic, moving past him as if to leave the room*) I . . . I think I'd better see if Mother needs me in the dining-room. There's rather a . . .

Brooke (*catching her arm, and turning to stop her*) Please don't go! Are you afraid of me, Margaret?

Meg (*arrested by his use, for the first time, of her Christian name*) How can I be afraid when you have been so kind to Mother and Father? I only wish I could thank you for it.

Brooke (*taking her hand gently*) Shall I tell you how?

Meg (*trying to withdraw her hand*) Oh, no, please don't . . . I'd rather you didn't . . . I . . .

Brooke I only want to know if you care for me a little. You see, I love you so much, Meg.

Meg (*trying to pull herself together and remember her carefully rehearsed speech*) Thank you, Mr Brooke, you are very kind, but I . . . (*she raises her eyes, looks into his, and weakens*) but I . . . but I don't know . . .

Brooke (*softly*) Will you try to find out? I want to know so desperately; for I can't go to work with any heart until I know just what your feelings are for me.

Meg (*struggling to resume her speech*) I'm not sure that I . . .

Brooke I'll wait; and, in the meantime, you could be learning to love me. Would you find that a very hard lesson, Meg?

Meg (*weakening again*) Not if I choose to learn it, but . . .

Brooke Please choose to learn. I love to teach, (*with a smile*) and this would be so much easier than German.

Meg (*striving to recover her earlier determination*) I . . . No . . . I think it would be better if we remained just friends as we were.

Brooke (*with surprise*) But, Meg, do you really mean . . .?

So preoccupied are they that neither has heard the front door open or the movement in the hall which heralds the arrival of Aunt March who now makes a sudden appearance in the archway

Meg Please, I don't want to say any more for the moment, I think . . . (*She turns away from him to be confronted by the sight of her formidable relative*) . . . Aunt March!

Aunt March Yes! Aunt March! I've come to see your father. My maid saw him coming out of the railroad station not an hour since and rushed home to tell me. So I got straight into the carriage and drove over here. (*Sensing the atmosphere, and looking suspiciously from one to the other*) What's all this, then? Since when have you been entertaining soldiers in this house?

Meg (*un-nerved and rather at a loss*) This is . . . er . . . this is Father's friend . . . I . . . Aunt March, I'm so surprised to see you!

Aunt March That's evident! (*Eyeing Brooke with growing disapproval*) And what has "Father's friend" been saying to you to make you look like a peony? There's mischief going on here, and I insist upon knowing what it is!

Meg We were just . . . talking. (*She turns to the equally embarrassed Brooke*) I think, perhaps, Father needs you, Mr Brooke.

Grateful for the chance to escape, Brooke bows hurriedly to both ladies, and exits quickly to the safety of the kitchen

Aunt March catches the name, and looks even more sharply at him as he disappears

Aunt March Brooke? That boy's tutor? Ah, I understand now! I know all about it. Jo blundered into a wrong message when she was reading one of your father's letters to me and I made her tell me the rest. You haven't gone and accepted him, child?

Meg (*very confused*) Hush! He'll hear. (*She starts to move*) I'll let Mother know that you've come.

Aunt March You'll stay right where you are! And don't "hush" me. I have something to say to you and I must free my mind on the matter at once. Tell me, do you mean to marry this Hook? (*She pauses, but, as there is no reply from Meg, continues the attack*) If you do, I want you to clearly understand that not one penny of my money will ever come to you.

Meg (*her blood rising*) I shall marry whom I please, Aunt March, and you may leave your money to any one you like.

Aunt March Highty-tighty! Is that the way you take my advice! You'll be sorry for it, by and by, when you've tried love in a cottage and know it to be a failure. There's little enough happiness to be found in poverty, miss!

Meg (*pointedly*) And does everyone find it with wealth, Aunt March?

Aunt March (*realizing that she must change her tactics*) Now, Meg, be reasonable and consider everything. You ought to marry well, and help your family. It's your duty to make a rich match, and it ought to be impressed upon you.

Meg Father and Mother don't think so; they like John even if he *is* poor.

Aunt March Your parents have no more worldly wisdom than my carriage horses.

Meg I can only say that I'm glad of it!

Aunt March This Rook is poor and has no rich relations to help him has he?

Meg No—but he has many warm friends.

Aunt March Huh! You can't live on friends however warm they may be; try it and see how cool they'll grow. What prospects has he?

Meg None yet; but Mr Laurence has promised to help him ...

Aunt March (*scornfully*) That won't last long! James Laurence is a crotchety old man, and not to be depended upon. So you intend to marry a man without money, position, or even prospects? I thought you had more sense, miss! You could do a great deal better, I am sure, if you'd only wait awhile.

Meg I couldn't do better if I waited half my life! John is good and wise and talented. He is willing to work and is sure to get on. Everyone likes and respects him and I'm proud to think that he cares for me—even though I'm poor and young and inexperienced.

Aunt March He knows that *you* have rich relations, that's the secret of his liking if I know anything!

Meg (*rounding on her*) Aunt March, how dare you say such a thing! John is above such meanness and I won't allow anyone to suggest otherwise. My John wouldn't marry for money any more than I would. We are both willing to work and we mean to wait until we can afford a little home of

our own. I'm not afraid of being poor for I've been happy so far and I
know I shall be happy with him because he loves me and I . . .

Aunt March (*rising*) Very well! I wash my hands of the whole affair! You are
a silly, wilful girl, and you have lost more than you know by this piece of
folly. You have upset and disappointed me. I haven't the heart to see your
father now, and you may tell him so! Don't expect anything from me
when you are married; your Mr Crooke's "warm friends" must take care
of you. I've done with you for ever!

She sweeps out in high dudgeon

The front door bangs behind her

Meg is left half-way between tears and laughter, but not for long

Brooke quickly re-appears and comes to her

Brooke (*taking her hand*) I couldn't help hearing, Meg. Thank you for
defending me—I'm very grateful to Aunt March for proving that you do
care for me a little!

Meg (*softly*) I didn't know just how much until she abused you.

Brooke (*taking her gently into his arms and lifting her face to his*) Then you
don't think you'll find your new lessons so difficult after all?

Meg (*almost in a whisper*) No, John.

*They embrace. Jo suddenly reappears, putting her head around the archway to
see why everything is so quiet after the storm. The sight which meets her eyes
transfixes her. For once in her life, she is speechless*

The lovers draw slightly apart—as yet blissfully unaware of their audience

Brooke Would you tell me that you love me, Meg?

Meg I love you, John.

They embrace again

*This is really too much for Jo; recovering her powers of speech she lets out a
great cry*

Jo Father! Mother! Oh, somebody do come quick! John Brooke is behaving
dreadfully—and Meg likes it!

*Mr March and Amy immediately appear in the archway, and move in to
congratulate Meg and Brooke. Amy brings two more glasses which she sets
down beside the others*

Mr March (*as he enters and crosses to shake Brooke warmly by the
hand*) Well, John, I am delighted! Nothing could give me greater
pleasure! (*He embraces Meg*)

*During the next speech Marmee enters from the dining-room and pauses
briefly to comfort the outraged Jo*

Amy We heard every word in the kitchen, but Father wouldn't let us come
in! He said he thought things were working themselves out for the best!

Marmee moves to join the others

   Jo, unable to stand any more of the general approval, exits to the kitchen

   Mr Laurence and Beth enter during the next speech

Marmee (*embracing Meg*) Meg, dear, you know that you have my warmest
blessing. (*She turns to Brooke and kisses him*) And, John, I cannot tell you
how happy this makes me!

Mr Laurence and Beth move forward to offer their congratulations

Mr Laurence My dear Brooke, many congratulations! You are a very
fortunate young fellow! (*He kisses Meg's hand*) My very best wishes to
you both! (*He turns to join Mr March and Marmee who have moved away*)

*As he continues to speak, Amy and Beth kiss their sister, and, after a little
hesitation, Brooke as well*

   To think that through his coming to us, this charming romance was
brought about.

*Mr March and Marmee respond as Hannah enters with a large glass bowl,
brimming with her own special brew of fruit punch, which she sets down on
the table. Amy moves to Hannah excitedly*

Amy Oh, Hannah! Isn't it exciting! Meg and Mr Brooke are engaged to be
married!

*Hannah crosses to Meg as Marmee moves to the table, and, with Amy's help,
starts to pour the punch into the glasses*

Hannah My! That Aunt March of yours is a tiresome old torment! I reckon
you stood up to her something proud, Miss Meg! (*She takes Meg's hand*)
Well, my lamb, I came here to nurse you as a babby, and I've seen you
grow to be a fine young woman. I'm as pleased for you now as I could
possibly be . . . and if this young man don't treat you proper, then I shall
be after him with my carpet beater!

Brooke (*laughing*) I hope there'll never be any need for you to resort to that,
Hannah!

Hannah Better not be, Mr John Brooke—I hit hard!

*Amid laughter, she moves back to the table to take up the tray of filled glasses
as soon as it is ready. She serves Mr Laurence first, then Mr March, followed
by Meg and Brooke. Beth and Amy take glasses from Marmee at the table.
Marmee takes a glass for herself just before the toast*

Amy Oh, Meg, when are we going to have the wedding? (*A sudden bright
idea hits her*) What about next week? Thursday would be a nice day to . . .

Mr March (*amid general amusement*) Amy, you mustn't let your enthusiasm
for excitement run away with you! I rather think that it will be a year or so
yet before you will be able to start planning your sister's wedding.

Amy (*appalled*) A year! But that is an age away! A wedding next week would have been such fun. Things are always so dreadfully dull just after Christmas.

Laurie enters in high spirits, moves forward to Meg, bows deeply, and, with a flourish, removes the small nosegay from his buttonhole which he presents to her

Laurie For the future Mrs John Brooke! I knew that Brooke would have it all his own way—he always does! When he makes up his mind to accomplish something, even if the sky falls, it's done!

Brooke (*laughing*) I'm much obliged for that recommendation! I take it as a good omen for the future, and invite you to the wedding, here and now!

Laurie (*crossing to the table to take up two glasses*) I'll come even if I'm at the ends of the earth. It would be worth the journey for the sight of Jo's face alone on that occasion!

Marmee Where is Jo?

Laurie (*moving up slightly to the archway*) In the kitchen. I've been trying to cheer her up, but she told me to leave her by herself.

Jo appears in the archway. She wears an expression of grim resignation

Laurie Ah, here is the lady! You don't look very festive, ma'am; pray, what is the matter?

Jo I still don't approve of the match, but I've made up my mind to bear it, and not say a word against it.

Amid laughter from the others, and cries of "Well done, Jo!"; "Make the best of it!"; "It's not as bad as all that, Jo!" etc. Jo moves down to shake hands with Brooke, and to kiss Meg. She then moves back to take a glass from Laurie. As the general mirth subsides, Mr March raises his glass

Mr March (*his glass raised first to Marmee*) Margaret, my little women (*he includes them all, and then turns to Mr Laurence, Laurie and Brooke*) dear friends, faithful Hannah, I give you a Christmas toast! To Peace, to the Family and this hearth and home, to lovers, (*he indicates Meg and Brooke*) to friendship. (*He turns to the Laurences*) In most families there comes, now and then, a year full of events; this has been just such a one for us. The joys have come close upon the anxieties, but it ends well after all! Let us drink to Christmas and the future!

Glasses are raised. There are cries of "Amen to that!" from Hannah; "Yes, to Christmas!", etc., from the younger folk; and "To peace and the New Year!" from the older ones. The toasts conclude and are followed by a gentle buzz of conversation as everyone fills in the few minutes left before Christmas dinner

Beth, already near her beloved piano, seats herself at it and, helped by Mr Laurence, begins to look through some music which lies on top of it. Amy moves to the cupboard to collect her sketch-book and pencils, and, then to find herself a suitable seat from which she can draw Meg and Brooke who, absorbed in each other, do not move. Meanwhile, Jo, still dejected, has moved to sit quietly in the chair below the fire. Laurie, whose eyes have not left her, joins her in an attempt to cheer her up

Laurie Don't be dismal, Jo! Meg is happy, and Brooke will fly around and get settled quite soon. Grandpa will help, I'm sure. And won't it be splendid to see Meg in a little home of her own?

Jo (*reluctantly*) I suppose so. It's just that it's so hard to give her up. I feel that I've lost my dearest friend.

Laurie But you don't give her up. You only go halves. (*His voice takes on a different, almost tender, note*) Besides, you've got me. I know I'm not good for much, but I'll stand by you all the days of my life—upon my word I will!

Jo (*softening*) I know you will, and I'm so grateful, Laurie. You're always such a comfort to me.

Laurie Then, just think of all the good times to come! Don't you wish you could take a look into the future?

Jo I think not, for I might see something sad—and everyone looks so happy now, that I don't believe things could be very much improved! (*She looks around the room*)

Meg and John, talking quietly together, are being sketched by Amy. Marmee is seated on the sofa, behind which stands Mr March; while Hannah, presiding over her punch-bowl, follows their eyes to the piano. Here, Beth, having found the music she sought, and with Mr Laurence to turn the pages for her, begins, very softly, to play the opening bars of "The First Nowell". Jo looks back at Laurie, leaning on her chair, and smiles. The music gradually gains strength

The Lights begin slowly to fade

CURTAIN

PRODUCTION NOTES

These notes are intended to help the less experienced director; in particular those working with school or youth groups who might feel drawn to doing a period play, but a little apprehensive in what seems to be a specialized field. Let me say at once that it's not really as difficult as it may appear!

Certainly, since this adaptation of *Little Women* was first published, an enormous number of directors in this category, often working with slender means and only limited stage facilities, have tackled it with great success and with equal enjoyment to both audience and cast alike.

Production

As a period piece, *Little Women* calls, of course, for careful attention to such things as movement, the wearing of costume (so that it looks like costume, and not fancy dress), and the manners and speech of a bygone age. Without thought for and preparation in these matters at rehearsal much is lost or never achieved in the final production.

The value of low-heeled shoes or dancing-pumps (ideally, the actual ones to be worn in performance) and long, practice skirts for the ladies, worn from an early stage in rehearsal, cannot be too heavily stressed. This makes for ease of movement and lack of consciousness of full skirts in performance which is not only desirable, but gives added confidence to those wearing them.

The keynote of the whole production should be simple sincerity, and every effort should be made to create the atmosphere of a warm, affectionate family. This intangible quality cannot be achieved entirely by the dialogue or specific moves; it is something that each member of the cast must feel and seek ways to express through the character which they portray. To the cast who has thought about the play and their parts, rather than just learned the lines, ideas will suggest themselves as rehearsals proceed. The director should do everything to encourage such lines of thought, as well as offer his or her own suggestions. Achieving this sense of family warmth and unity does enrich and add dimension to the final production in performance.

The contrast between the characters, especially of the four girls, should be brought out to give variety and life not only to the parts, but to the play as a whole. There can be, of course, no better guide to a complete understanding of all the characters than by a study of the original novel. It is more than just a good idea to get the cast to read it before rehearsals begin.

The period and the costumes lend themselves to attractive grouping, and particular use may be made of this at the opening of nearly all the scenes, and at many other moments throughout the play. The visual and pictorial possibilities are endless.

A good pace is desirable throughout, and simple, straightforward playing is all that is required in the more tender scenes; anything approaching the mawkishly sentimental or beautifully tragic should be avoided at all costs as it will kill these passages stone dead, and make your audience restless or embarrassed—or both.

The opening of each new scene should be lifted and not allowed to drag, so that the audience's interest and attention is immediately recaptured. Ideally, scenes should be divided by the fading of the lights in and out of a black-out; bringing in the front curtain each time is inclined to cut the evening into a series of one-act plays. However, for groups working with limited stage facilities, the use of the front curtain may be unavoidable. Either way, it is vital that the pauses between the scenes should be kept as brief as possible.

It is necessary, therefore, for members of the cast, who are left on stage at the end of a scene, to clear quickly and—above all—quietly during the break before the next scene, whether it be in a black-out or not, and for those who are to open the next scene to take their places with equal speed and silence. This is quite simple to do and can be achieved, literally, in a matter of seconds, but it does require some rehearsal, and for the on-coming members of the cast to be standing by ready to take up their positions.

To prevent wholesale confusion during a change-over it is a good idea for those concluding a scene to clear first before anyone else sets foot on stage, and for the backstage crew to keep their activities on stage to an absolute minimum during the change. The on-coming cast can be rehearsed in bringing on any new props (such as the tea-tray for Act I, Scene 3), and retiring members in removing props that are finished with, but which have not been removed in the course of the action of the play. Backstage staff should be waiting immediately in the wings to relieve the cast of these props as they leave the stage.

On a small stage, in particular, this system removes the danger of any clash—both physical and temperamental—between cast and property people struggling to get things in place. Too many bodies on stage at moments like this only make for short tempers and long scene changes.

As a scheme it works well, but it does require adequate rehearsal and the discipline of everyone working together swiftly and quietly. The flow of the action will not be broken if the scene changes are kept to a handful of seconds (as they can be), and covered with curtain music.

The use of an American accent by an inexperienced cast is debatable. Too often the harsher notes of the mid-West or the Bronx—culled from a half-digested diet of television cop and cowboy films—are churned out by English tongues as being "American". The New England accent is a gentle one, and one might reasonably suppose that in the 1860s it was, perhaps, even gentler—especially in educated circles. If, therefore, a light accent can be achieved by the cast—and maintained—it will, of course, add authenticity to the whole, but if the sense of what is being said begins to get lost in a welter of distorted vowels then it's probably as well to play it with no accent at all. The director must decide!

Setting

The setting can be considerably modified from that described without any real loss of dramatic effect. The scene is, after all, a simple parlour and not a grand drawing-room. Its old-fashioned charm should be its essential quality.

The archway at the back with the hall and stairs beyond is an attractive and useful feature as it offers three definite exits (i.e. upstairs, off right to the kitchen, and off left to the dining-room and front door), but it is not essential to the plot or action, and can be dispensed with on a shallow stage where an exit upstage centre is difficult to arrange. In this case the exit to the hall should be above the fireplace in the wall at stage right.

Similarly, the window upstage left can also be simplified, if necessary, to an ordinary sash-window, but a small bow or bay-window, if it can be contrived, does give added interest and character to the room.

Patterned walls in a not too obtrusive design give a better period effect than plain ones. The use of a dado with patterned walls above it was fashionable at the time, and creates a greater feeling of space. But, whatever is chosen, the end result must have a comfortable 'lived-in' appearance. Any suggestion of a bright, freshly-decorated look should be avoided at all costs.

Lighting

The period atmosphere and the many changing dramatic moods of the play can be heightened and enriched by imaginative lighting, but, once more, the director will be limited by the lighting facilities at his or her disposal. As a brief general note, it should be remembered when lighting evening scenes that this was the period of the flattering golden glow of lamplight. But, in any case, all scenes should be lit as softly and romantically as possible. Harsh, white light is not suitable.

Furnishings

Furniture should be early Victorian (circa 1840/60) with, ideally, a piece or two of earlier American "Colonial". Directors working on a small budget will have to settle for what they can beg or borrow, of course, but, even so, they should keep an eye open for pieces with charm and elegance.

It is the home of a comfortable, middle-class family in reduced circumstances. The furnishings are meant to be good and well-cared for; whilst a worn, faded look is acceptable, anything drab or downright shabby would strike the wrong note.

Round tables of varying diameter were popular at this time, and are useful on stage as they take up less room and are easier to walk around than square ones. Difficulty in obtaining the size required can be overcome by having a top made from the cheapest materials, and placing it on an existing base—square or round. It need only be rough-finished and, covered with a floor-length cloth, no one will be the wiser.

The piano should be set downstage left during the interval between Acts I and II. However, if restricted space makes it difficult to introduce additional furniture once the set is up, or to store it backstage until required, it can stay permanently in position on stage, and be hidden during Act I by one of those scrapbook screens which were familiar features in homes of the period. In the original production a small table-piano of about 1830 was used; this was exactly right in every way, and a very lucky find in a local music shop, but a later, upright piano, providing it is not too modern in appearance, would do equally well.

Whilst on this subject, it might be as well to mention that, if the actresses playing Beth or Marmee are unable to play the piano, a ghost-pianist, off-stage at another piano, works more successfully than using taped music, especially when accompanying the singing. Again, it needs careful rehearsal, but by "striking a chord" before starting to "play", the actress should be able to follow the ghost-pianist without fear of making a false start.

A tremendous sense of period can be achieved for the set by careful attention to detail in such things as ornaments, pictures, lamps, cushion-covers (patchwork, bead or woollen embroidery, crochet, appliqué work, etc.), china, books, chenille tablecloths, antimacassars, potted plants and so on.

Costumes

The costumes should be kept fairly simple. Apart from the fact that the family is passing through hard times, clothes, at that period, were made to last much longer than they are today. Furthermore, the action of the play covers only one year, so there is no need for numerous changes of costume.

Woollen homespun gowns are suitable for Act I (with the obvious exception of the party dresses which should also be quite simple), with a change to light, cotton dresses for Act II, and a return to the Act I dresses for Act III.

Shawls were very much in vogue—both for the warmth they afforded and their considerable decorative value. They came in all sizes from the very large all-enveloping to the very small shoulder-covering, and in all materials from heavy wool to fine lace. Considerable variety can be given to the same costume by making use of this fashion; for example, in Act I, Marmee might well pull on a warm, knitted shawl to read by the fire, whilst the girls are at the Gardiners' party, and don a pretty, silk one over the same dress when entertaining Mr Laurence to tea.

Aunt March's clothes should be as rich and elaborate as possible in marked contrast to the rest of the family, and the Laurences must also give the impression of wealth in their attire.

Most costumiers—even relatively small firms—should be able to dress the show without difficulty. However, for the enterprising group who elects to make its own costumes there is a wide range of books to help them. For quick, easy reference Lucy Barton's *Historic Costume for the Stage*, long accepted as a standard work on the subject, remains a rich source of information with very useful sections on cutting and reproducing costumes, suitable materials, application of decoration, accessories and so on.

Hair

Careful attention to the matter of hair-styles is very important in any period play, and *Little Women* is no exception. No matter how accurate a costume may be, if the hair-style doesn't match it the whole effect will be wrong.

Wigs are by no means essential, and excellent results can be achieved by dressing the actresses' own hair—using matching hairpieces where necessary. For the older characters there is less of a problem. The larger part of Marmee's hair will be concealed under a lace house-cap; Hannah, too, will have most of her hair caught up under a mob-cap, and Aunt March never removes her bonnet. For the girls, however, a definite and different style should be thought out to suit each character and to give contrast and visual interest. The local public library should be able to provide a good reference book to give inspiration in detail, but Lucy Barton's book, already mentioned, will supply good general information on the subject.

The business of Jo's hair being loosened in Act I, and cut off in Act II can be tackled in various ways—depending on the actress playing the part. Assuming that her hair is the right colour—chestnut—and cut quite short, the problem can be overcome with a carefully matched hairpiece pinned firmly in place so that it can be released from the hairnet in the first scene, and removed altogther for the scenes after she is supposed to have had it cut off. If the reverse applies, and the actress has long hair, then a matching short-haired wig is needed for the change-over. If the hair is not the right colour, or of a length which is neither one thing nor the other, then the only solution is two wigs—one short, one long.

Meg's scorched curls in Act I can be made by wrapping ordinary crepe-hair in paper, and pinning them lightly in place with hairpins or grips. Jo, by holding her hand in front of them in a perfectly natural way as she applies the curlers, hides the fact that she is not really touching them at all. A light tug pulls them away at the right moment giving the desired effect.

Music
The right music in the right form adds considerably to any production—creating mood and atmosphere as well as a feeling for a particular period. In this instance it helps, also, to maintain those qualities, provide continuity between the scenes, and keep the flow of the production unbroken.

In the original production, "Home, Sweet Home" and other contemporary melodies taped from those large, perforated-steel discs which preceded the gramophone achieved a charming musical-box sound and made ideal curtain music. However, simple piano arrangements of the same sort of music—either taped or live—would be just as effective.

The piano piece which Beth is playing at the opening of Act II does not have to be Brahm's Cradle Song, any other popular piano solo of the time may be used—such as "The Last Rose of Summer" or "The Bluebells of Scotland". Incidentally, only the last few bars are required; it should not be allowed to develop into a musical interlude as this will slow down the action and make the opening of the second act sluggish.

"O, Worship the King"—a favourite mid-nineteenth century hymn—is an appropriate choice for "Father's favourite" at the close of Act II.

In conclusion
Louisa Alcott describes, in an early chapter in the original novel, the
theatrical activities of the March girls as they prepare a family play for
Christmas. They had their problems too . . .
"Not rich enough to afford any great outlay . . . the girls put their wits to
work, and—necessity being the mother of invention—made whatever they
needed."
And after the performance? Well . . .
"Tumultuous applause followed".
What further incentive is needed?

PETER CLAPHAM

FURNITURE AND PROPERTY LIST

Directors will, of course, adapt to their own particular requirements and stage limitations. Essential items of furniture are marked with an asterisk; other items were purely decorative to dress the stage and help create a sense of period. These may be included or discarded at the director's discretion.

ACT I

Scene 1

On stage: Low, upholstered sewing-chair DR*

Upholstered wing-chair or armchair (**Marmee**'s) above fireplace*

To R of it: small round table.* *On it:* chenille cloth, oil-lamp, framed pictures, book (**Marmee**'s)

Portrait of George Washington over fireplace

Mantelpiece. *On it:* drape, clock, ornaments, handbell, picture of Mr March

In front of fire: brass fender, fire irons, coal scuttle, bellows, hearth-rug, toasting-fork, kettle-holder

Upstage archway: drapes

Hallway beyond arch: hall-stand, occasional chair

Upstage: cabinet-bookcase.* *In it:* decanter of wine, wine glasses, drawing-pad and materials (**Amy**'s)

Footstool

Windows up L: lace curtains, draped, heavy curtains

In front of window: round table.* *On it:* chenille cloth, small, decorated Christmas tree in a pot

Stage C: sofa.* *Above it:* round table.* *On it:* chenille cloth, workbasket with dark blue knitted sock on needles (**Jo**'s). *Under it:* two, small, dining-chairs*

Off stage: **Marmee**'s slippers (**Amy**)

Tray. *On it:* teacup and saucer, milk-jug, sugar basin, plate of bread for toasting (**Hannah**)

Invitation in an envelope (**Hannah**)

Teapot with hot tea (**Hannah**)

Letter in an envelope (**Marmee**)

Basket of food covered with a white cloth (**Jo**)

Five small packages wrapped in white tissue-paper and tied with coloured ribbons (**Jo**)

Two bottles of wine wrapped in white tissue-paper, a bunch of hothouse flowers wrapped the same (**Laurie**)

Personal: **Meg:** dark blue, knitted sock on needles

Jo: book, hair net

Beth: box from which the Christmas decorations have been taken

Amy: small silver star for the top of the Christmas tree

Little Women

SCENE 2

Strike: Tea tray, presents, bottles of wine

Set: **Meg**'s evening cloak on the sofa (brought on by **Meg** in the Black-out)
Meg's gloves and evening bag on c table (brought on by **Meg**)
Comb and hand-mirror on c table (brought on by **Beth**)

Off stage: Lace handkerchief (**Amy**)
Curling-tongs (**Amy**)
Cloak, gloves, evening bag containing bon-bons wrapped in a handkerchief
Small woollen shawl, book (**Marmee**)
Small tray. *On it:* bandage, lint, towel, bottle of linament etc. (**Marmee**)

Personal: **Meg:** curling papers in hair, new ribbon, pearl brooch, new slippers
Jo: scorch-marked dress
Amy: curling papers, peg on nose

SCENE 3

Strike: Tray with bandages etc

Set: Large tray with four cups and saucers, a silver teapot, milk-jug, sugar basin, fruit cake, plate of cookies and other confectionery

Off-stage: Small posy of flowers (**Brooke**)
Lady's white glove (**Brooke**)

Personal: **Marmee:** silk shawl

ACT II

SCENE 1

Strike: Tea tray, Christmas tree and decorations

Set: Furnishings as for Act I, but rearranged for warmer weather, Christmas tree replaced with a potted plant
Piano DL. *On it:* sheet music, letter in an envelope
Ink-well, pen and paper in bookcase upstage (**Jo**)

Off stage: Newspaper, shawl, new bonnet (**Jo**)

Personal: **Marmee:** sewing

SCENE 2

Set: Playing cards for **Amy** and **Beth**
Pen, paper and envelopes. Ink-well in cupboard (**Jo**)

Off-stage: Bowl of roses (**Meg**)
Bonnet, shawl, gloves (**Jo**)
Telegram in an envelope (**Jo**)
Two bottles of wine—unwrapped (**Amy**)
Trunk (**Hannah** and **Laurie**)
Small portmanteau, overcoat and hat (**Brooke**)
Small tray. *On it:* teapot, milk-jug, sugar basin, cup and saucer (**Meg**)

Basket of food covered with a cloth (**Amy** and **Beth**)
Cup and saucer (**Beth**)
Parcel of medical supplies wrapped in brown paper and string (**Jo**)
Roll of dollar bills (**Jo**)
Lock of hair wrapped in a handkerchief (**Jo**)

ACT III

SCENE 1

Strike: Tea tray

Set: Furnishings as for Act I
           Meg's cloak and bonnet on hallstand
           Telegram by the clock on the mantelpiece
           Decanter of wine and glasses in the bookcase (**Laurie**)
           Drawing pad containing Amy's will.
             Drawing materials in cupboard (**Amy**)
           Inkstand, pen and paper on the table C (**Jo**)

Off stage: Small portmanteau, **Amy**'s bonnet, cloak and gloves (**Jo**)

Personal: **Meg:** duster, apron
            Amy: apron

SCENE 2

Set: As for Scene 1. Return **Amy**'s drawing materials to the bookcase

Personal: **Meg:** cloak and bonnet

SCENE 3

Set: Small decorated Christmas tree in a pot on the table in front of the
             window
           Evergreens and winter flowers to decorate the room
           Small scroll on the table C (**Jo**)

Off stage: Tray. *On it:* eight glasses and two glasscloths (**Hannah**)
            Travelling rug (**Beth**)
            Two glasses (**Amy**)
            Tray. *On it:* large bowl of fruit punch (**Hannah**)

Personal: **Brooke:** long cloak, muffler, gloves, hat
            Mr March: long cloak, muffler
            Laurie: Nosegay-buttonhole

LIGHTING PLOT

This is a basic lighting plot which can be enlarged and embellished to suit individual productions. Please see Production Notes

Property fittings required: fire effect, lamps in hall, by Marmee's chair and on the C table. Elsewhere as needed

All scenes should open and close with slow fades from or to a Black-out

ACT I

To open: Black-out

Cue 1	After the Curtain rises *Lights fade up on the March sisters*	(Page 1)
Cue 2	**Marmee** and **Hannah** laugh quietly together as they exit *Lights fade slowly to Black-out*	(Page 14)
Cue 3	As Scene 2 opens *Lights fade up on* **Beth** *and* **Meg**	(Page 14)
Cue 4	Marmee moves to the fire *Lights fade to Black-out for a few moments, then come up on* **Marmee** *in her chair by the fire*	(Page 18)
Cue 5	**Jo:** "Christopher Columbus!" *Lights fade to Black-out*	(Page 23)
Cue 6	As Scene 3 opens *Lights fade up on a warm sunshine effect through the window on* **Marmee** *and* **Mr Laurence**	(Page 23)
Cue 7	**Brooke** looks at the evening glove *Lights fade slowly to Black-out*	(Page 27)

ACT II

To open: Black-out

Cue 8	After Curtain rises *Lights fade up* **Marmee, Hannah, Amy** *and* **Beth**. *Summer sunshine*	(Page 28)
Cue 9	**Amy** moves towards the stairs *Lights fade slowly to Black-out*	(Page 35)
Cue 10	As Scene 2 opens *Lights up on* **Beth** *and* **Amy**	(Page 35)
Cue 11	**Mr Laurence** comforts **Marmee** *Lights fade to Black-out for a few moments, then come up on* **Laurie** *and* **Hannah**	(Page 40)

Cue 12   As the singing continues   (Page 46)
           Lights fade gently

ACT III

To open: Lights fade up on **Meg** and **Jo**

Cue 13   **Amy** exits forlornly   (Page 55)
           Lights fade to Black-out

Cue 14   As Scene 2 opens   (Page 55)
           Lights fade up to lamp light shining in hall

Cue 15   **Jo** turns up lamp c   (Page 55)
           Bring up covering lights

Cue 16   **Laurie** draws the curtains aside   (Page 59)
           Snow effect on the window

Cue 17   **Laurie:** "She's home again!"   (Page 59)
           Lights fade to Black-out

Cue 18   As Scene 3 opens   (Page 59)
           Winter sunshine streams through the window

Cue 19   As the music gains strength   (Page 73)
           Lights fade slowly to Black-out

EFFECTS PLOT

ACT I

Cue 1   **Meg:** "You're a dear and nothing else."   (Page 3)
Clock strikes six

Cue 2   **Marmee:** "... in case Aunt March wishes to speak to you."   (Page 9)
Door bell rings loudly and autocratically

Cue 3   **Marmee** begins to move towards the kitchen   (Page 12)
Door bell rings

Cue 4   As the Lights come up on **Marmee** in her chair by the fire   (Page 18)
Clock strikes ten

Cue 5   As **Marmee** continues reading   (Page 18)
Carriage approachs and then stops

Cue 6   **Marmee** and **Mr Laurence** pass out of sight   (Page 25)
Clock chimes the half-hour

ACT II

Cue 7   **Mr Laurence:** "... and even approves—with reservations."   (Page 27)
Door bell rings

Cue 8   **Laurie:** "... I'll go down the road and see if she's coming."   (Page 40)
Door bell rings

ACT III

Cue 9   As **Hannah** and **Beth** move to the stairs   (Page 50)
Door bell rings

Cue 10   **Marmee:** "Jo and I will do the glasses"   (Page 60)
Door bell rings

MADE AND PRINTED IN GREAT BRITAIN BY
LATIMER TREND & COMPANY LTD PLYMOUTH
MADE IN ENGLAND